ALSO BY KAREN GOLDMAN

THE ANGEL BOOK

ANGEL VOICES

ANGEL
ENCOUNTERS

❖

True Stories of Divine Intervention

❖

BY KAREN GOLDMAN

Illustrations by Patricia Languedoc

❖

SIMON & SCHUSTER
New York • London • Toronto • Sydney • Tokyo• Singapore

SIMON & SCHUSTER
Rockefeller Center
1230 Avenue of the Americas
New York, NY 10020

Text copyright © 1995 by Karen Goldman
Illustrations copyright © 1995 by Patricia Languedoc
All rights reserved,
including the right of reproduction
in whole or in part in any form.

Simon & Schuster and colophon are registered trademarks
of Simon & Schuster Inc.

DESIGNED BY CHARLES KRELOFF

Manufactured in the United States of America
10 9 8 7 6 5 4 3 2 1
Library of Congress Cataloging-in-Publication Data is available.

ISBN 0-684-80184-1

Dedication

This book is dedicated to the magnificent angels who visit this world and all sincere souls who leave the door open...To ordinary people whose lives overflow with angel stories...To those selfless human beings who devote their lives to becoming more angelic, for whom the sun of love never sets, even after they die...those hearts who carry their love so deep inside themselves that everything they do and say comes from that remarkable place...and always to the beautiful "angel" that wants to come out in all of us.... To Uncle Barney; Pop-pop; Moish Glassman, who went to Heaven this year; Jade Earl, a good-hearted and special little girl I am proud to call my friend; Alan Pollak; Sam Milgrim—my adorable stepbrother; Basile Burwell, my eleventh-grade writing teacher; Robert Adams; Self-Realization Fellowship; Lester Levinson and the Sedona Institute, teachers of the Release technique, in Phoenix, Arizona.

...To all the brave and sweetly generous people who share their most treasured and private experiences with the Divine and the glow that we feel because of it. . . .

Acknowledgments

My special thanks to Al Lowman, my perfect agent, and B. G. Dillworth, his perfect second-in-command; Collette Goldman, my sister-in-law—the writer; Annie Helm; Thomas Campbell; Todd Felderstein; Andrea Cagan; Ed Astrin; Philip Waters; Jim Ezrine; and my angelic Nan…for all their assistance, love, and kindness.

Contents

RESCUES

HEALINGS

III ETERNAL ADVICE *232*

Angel Gifts

In Spring, the angels sing for passions found, while ladies
Hold to one another for fear the angels steal their beauty . . .

And gentlemen pronounce the words of love, while overhead a Cupid with
Perfection's bow attempts a "fate."
But if the challenge hurts to tell, the angels simply whisper… "All is well!"

Before the fancy dance begins, an angel picks a fruit and settles in.
With flowers boldly drifting down through space,
The angels hold our gentle hands in grace.

They minister in rosy splendor.
The color gold resounds like trumpet bursts about their heads.
In visions, in halo light, in remarkable poise they go and often blend in flowers.

They answer prayers. They study love. And speak in elegance.
The bells of joy are struck each hour by heavenly hands.

Simple presents tied with flower ribbons, streamers of light…angel gifts…
Little voices, singing treasures, holding now the future bright…
"Stop to listen, precious one. Only now begins the fun!"

12

I

What Is an Angel Encounter?

Angel Encounters are tales of celestial rescue, "magic," heroism, and blessings in the form of selfless behavior, "in the nick of time" aid, outstanding generosity, magical support, fortuitous coincidence, life-changing encouragement, or "adoption" by a compassionate guardian, whether physical or ethereal, who ensures one's safety through hazardous circumstances.

An angel encounter is an inner crossing of paths with the Divine. It is a meeting with the eternal celestial Guide and Source. Whenever we approach Heaven, by intention, by openness, or simply by grace, we meet our angels halfway.

Their form may be anything at all: a being of light appearing at the corner of our eye, a voice from nowhere directing us to safety, or a messenger from above who appears in our life at just the right moment—perhaps sans the wings. Or it may be a stranger whose actions remind us of lofty places in ourselves, long abandoned; someone who fulfills that much-needed place in our history so that a heart can mend, a blessing can be manifest more easily, an important action can be taken that couldn't have been

by any other means. We who are attuned know that these are all angel stories, touching our innermost nature as if with a magic wand, awakening all our brightest hopes, our unsung dreams and wishes, and washing clean our very souls.

These are stories of the mundane and the extraordinary, told by ordinary people and remarkable ones, about the moments when Heaven dipped right into their own experience and somehow made them greater than they believed themselves to be.

Those of us who have come to believe in angels all have our own stories. We have been rescued from the dangers of contemporary living, guided to undeniable truths, inspired to become more than we ever thought we could be. We have been visited by forms of love and guidance that we never knew existed, recognition that, like rainwater, nourishes our hearts and souls with tender relief and a sense of newfound humor that makes us weep our own divine and salty tears.

The people to whom these encounters happened defined them as angel stories. No one had to be pushed or probed. There was no effort in their responses when these people were questioned. There were no apologies or hesitations once they began talking. "This is what happened," they begin, and out comes a tale of true love. They are articulate and clear: No mumbling or inventing. No apologizing, no bragging. Once they know someone is interested enough, they just tell.

While reading or listening to angel stories, we must be careful not to judge. The stories contain elements that may disturb, as well as inspiring food for the soul. These stories are told by the people to whom they happened, in their own words. It is not our job to judge their lives, their moral precepts, or their understanding any more than the angels have. If Heaven felt them worthy, we must put aside our prejudgments in order to hear.

Nearly all these people I know or have at least met. These people are healthy, ordinary human beings with families, careers, jobs, homes, social lives, and political opinions. They are as real as people get. Yet these are the stories that they generally don't tell...the stories that are too precious, too extraordinary to be believed.

It is not my job to argue religions, beliefs, saviors, theology, the "chosen," the "damned," the devil, sin, or Hell. I report about angels in a nondenominational and all-inclusive way, as I feel called to. Likewise, for the purpose of this book I've divided the stories into healings, visions, and rescues. Yet in a subtle way, every angel encounter is a healing and a rescue that increases our vision.

The purpose of sharing angel stories is to show us that we are each special, and not special at all; to publicly acclaim the divine ones who minister to each of us irrespective of our earthly differences; and to openly join hands with one another through our common bond with Heaven.

Angels are right in our own neighborhoods, in our own field of experience, visiting people next door and right down the street, people who are living with us and doing business with us. No one has to look very far to find proof of an angel. I started asking people, "Do you have an angel story?" at my dentist's office, the hairdresser, people I met on the telephone through business, friends, and acquaintances. How often I heard, "Yes! As a matter of fact...!"

These are the stories of friends and friends of friends. I didn't have to look far to find them. Much to my own amazement, I've

discovered that rather than few and far between, angel encounters are happening all around us and that very normal people everywhere have been touched by something or someone that has left them with tremendous faith.

Some angel stories are subtle. They're particular quiet moments that could be discarded as fantasy, easily dismissed as wishful thinking or as the sweet, sad delusions of sweet, sad people. But rather than labeling, remember that angels speak through the heart to those listening.

An angel story told is a messenger in story clothing. When we tell our stories, we, too, become "angels"—angelic messengers, transmitting the presence of the Divine to one another. We share our stories so that, in their telling, we can promote and attract the miraculous power of God and His angels.

Heaven approves of our sharing. That is evident in the charge of energy, like spiritual electricity, exchanged between us. Chills, goose bumps, tears, and laughter pass from Heaven to storyteller, from storyteller to listener. We are all messengers when we reveal our own special experiences.

Lots of people all over the planet are finding true spiritual happiness and guidance as we're forced to go within for answers and comfort. For many people it's the world situation or illness that will do it. But for all of us, the very existence of angels will often answer questions we cannot get answered anywhere else.

Everyday angels are becoming more real to people, and the reality of the love and bonding possible is continually growing. Angel stories can make us happier people if we let them.

But who are these spiritual creatures, these forces for good, these beings of light? The unsure are stepping forward, wanting to hear more, and the "touched" are speaking out. It is a good day for the angels.

As you read these accounts of angelic visitations you can draw your own conclusions, or better still, don't draw any at all. Take this as an angelfeast. Eat it all up, and spit out whatever you don't want. You may forget the stories and the story-tellers…but once you encounter an angel for yourself, your life will be changed forever.

The stories in this book were collected during the 1993–94 period from personal and radio interviews and mail-ins. I feel a great love for everyone who wrote to me and for all the story-tellers, and I also appreciate the generosity and trust they felt in revealing these precious moments to me and to you.

It is through such generosity that we can become a freer, happier world.

Making Themselves Known

There have always been people who wholeheartedly believe in angels, who collect their figures and images on cards and figurines, who carve them into architecture, incorporating them into their lives and the lives of their children. Lovers and poets throughout history have long addressed their angels and Cupid, imagined to be circling above, with his bow and arrow poised, for advice. All through the centuries, these people have been waiting for the rest of us to catch up...to catch on.

They are not bothered by our lack of faith but wish us the same happiness that they feel at the sight of a cherub or winged archangel or sprite, whether made of plaster, paint, or the heavenly substance of light. They are not kooks but remarkably sweet people with a divine sense of humor, an uncluttered imagination, and a little extra faith.

Angels have received tremendous publicity recently. They have been featured in *Time* magazine, *Newsweek*, *The Wall Street Journal*, *USA Today*, and many other publications. They have been the topic of recent books and films, newspaper articles, and talk shows, and have even been featured on CNN, with broadcasts to 140 countries worldwide. TV networks are doing a variety of angel projects, from specials to weekly series and interview shows. Angel books are being translated and published in numerous countries throughout the world.

In recent years, perhaps more than ever before, angels are making themselves known. They are allowing us to know them on their own angelic terms, but in our own context. Only a small percentage of people consider angels to be figments of religious fanatics' imaginations anymore. Our limiting concepts about angels are dissolving.

Publishers and producers are finding to their amazement that interest in the topic of angels is not waning but increasing in a mind-boggling way. On a world scale, big business, world politics, and mainstream religion are all acknowledging the new wave of angelic influence.

It seems that with the millennium approaching, the angels have launched a new campaign. They have broken out of the religious stronghold and are merging into public consciousness, between church steeples, temples, and mosques, out in the streets, and in the homes and workplaces and entertainment capitals of the world.

Angels have a role; it is not a new one, perhaps, but it is more critical now than ever before. Because a world of people is finally seeking answers, angels are reappearing in our culture, emerging from the dusty old books of the seminaries and religious libraries, out into the sunlight of modern needs. Using ordinary spokespeople as beacons of hope, they are emerging as our long-forgotten heroes and friends, as messengers of a new day. We all need a new day, and the angels are here now, to guide us. They are making themselves known, available, easy to discover...because we have asked for them.

Why They Are Here

Angel encounters answer the question "Are we really just stuck here together on this little blue planet, spinning through space, trying to survive? Are we mere human ants working and procreating before the great absent eye of a dark and silent universe? Is our search for meaning the only search we have left in this age of advanced technology?"

What was meaningful centuries ago has paled in the light of our ability to communicate instantaneously with billions of people, to fly to the planets and walk the moon, to jet across oceans, entertaining ourselves with films and cordless telephones while working on our laptop computers. Undeniably, we have advanced beyond the dreams of old into a new physical reality. Our doctors can even bring people back from the "dead."…But emotionally, psychologically, and spiritually, have we moved so very much?

How can we explain our new circumstances to our souls? Where does God fit into the new picture? Is it His world or is it ours now? If we are so advanced, why do we still have wars and nuclear stockpiles? Why are we still depressed and angry, facing social upheaval and the threat of economic collapse? Why does injustice still abound throughout the world?

Throughout the history of the world, the most brilliant and, often, the most fulfilled and exceptional people have sought the connection between Heaven and earth, between imagination and reality, between the human soul and the soul of nature, between our individual hearts and the heart of the Divine.

Human beings have spiritual needs at every moment. We have hopes, dreams, and spiritual hungers that propel our imaginations and our actions. Yet the material world largely ignores the spiritual essence upon which it exists. That is what our angels are here for. Angels begin to address our deeper needs by punching pinholes of light in the life that we take so much for granted so much of the time.

The miraculous, the mysterious, and the mystical are in demand now, but too often we call on them only in times of physical danger. When the bills can't get paid, when the car is careening out of control, when the airplane starts to drop, when riots or earthquakes break out, then we suddenly remember God. At those critical times, we shock ourselves, suddenly realizing how far we've been living from our Source. Yet we do not need to wait for disaster to strike.

We can recognize the natural yearnings of our souls, the essence of our deepest desires, now. We can begin to wake ourselves up today, emerge from our unconsciousness effortlessly, discover our own higher purpose and save ourselves a world of grief. As an encouragement, we would be wise to take time to notice that there are small, subtle, and deeply guiding miracles of love happening, little angel encounters taking place, with or without our awareness, all the time, to all of us.

Angels are not a "New Age" phenomenon. They are not a commercial product, an offbeat trend, or a mere revival of a cultural phenomenon. Angels are not the stuff of cults, imaginary genies, or wish collectors. Angels are not subject to the corruption of our thinking, our sarcasm or cynicism, our misplaced resentments or destructive tendencies. They are not affected by our egotistic struggles at all. Angels are not a fad. They have been around as long as mankind—even longer. Historically, the sharing of angel encounters has always been dramatic, uplifting, and fun. Angels are not about to disappear.

More often than we care to admit, we all happen upon unanswered questions and impossible riddles. Even for the scientifically minded, the atheist, and the one who regards himself in a seat of great power or authority there are age-old questions, seeds of doubt, and cracks in understanding that just never seem to be resolved. Even for those steely ones who take life at face value, there are still cravings, unfulfilled longings, and all-too-human quandaries that erupt at critical moments. We are forced to our knees, revealing that hidden, tender part that begs for understanding, for a truly nonjudgmental love and relief from the painful distance the soul too often feels from the Source of everything.

It is not difficult to believe that something has gone terribly wrong today. We are suffering at the hands of negative thinking and destructive influences generated and left unchecked by the egos of a few. These are special times. Technology has moved us beyond our capabilities to protect ourselves. The media has given us information systems we cannot emotionally cope with.

For the first time in recorded history, our environment has succumbed to our influence and is beginning to lash back at us. The earth is not really big anymore, but neither are we. There are planetary symptoms of "dis-ease," like pollution, holes in the ozone layer, and changes in weather. We have the sad intelligence of nuclear weapons at our disposal, with potential to destroy the world as we know it. And although we've advanced technologi-

cally, man's inhumanity to man has not been eliminated.

We need a spiritual lift—a big one—to break us out of our
ruts, something to wake us up and get us out of the conflictual
mentality from which we're suffering as a world. We each need
an angel, or a big flock of them. But mainly, we need a couple of
miracles and a sure way to feel safe again. We need our faith
restored in the goodness of our Maker, in one another as human
beings, in love, and in our own freedom and our ability to make
better choices.

This is a time for miracles, a time for intervention…This is
clearly a time…for **angels.**

Trying to Explain a Miracle

*P*eople always speak in reverent tones when they tell their
angel stories. Angel stories are never told from pride or silliness.
No matter how dramatic, the experience doesn't encourage
bragging or boasting or an attitude of superiority. Angel stories
are humbling…moving, and always very beautiful. They are told
with complete trust, with gentleness and love. (Or they are not
told at all.) They are intimately shared stories of extraordinarily
private experiences with the Divine.

They are told with gratitude. They are told with confidence.
They are told with tears rolling down our faces. They are told in
such a way that one knows that they are expected to be
believed. They are told in real, unmasked voices. They are true
stories; personal stories.…They are stories of a greater truth

24

discovered and accepted. They are stories of the undeniable reality and wonder of the truth of Heaven.

Some angel stories you may recognize as similar to something that's happened to you. You may have your own angel story or two up your sleeve in your own spiritual closet, half-forgotten.

The mind tends not to remember what it cannot explain. Some extraordinary and angelic moments we have experienced in our lives may emerge from our own subconscious when we enlighten it with an acceptable category to place them in. Under this new definition—angel encounters—our hidden angel-touched self may simply confess.

Some find instant recognition—the tears will flow. Your own angel vision may be described in detail by a stranger. You may find yourself saying, "Yes, yes, that's right," as you review those holy moments when the Divine Ones graced your presence. You will feel the similarities. You will join hands with others you have never met and know you have shared an authentic piece of Heaven with another soul. You will instantly know that you are not alone—that no one is. Not only do we have angels, but we have each other as well. Angels remind us that we are copilots here, connected equals in the eyes of the Divine.

The stories and the people and especially the angels speak for themselves. It is hoped that, by sharing and listening, many more of us will receive the same gifts that the angels have been kind enough to give a few.

Perhaps it is wisest to just listen and let the stories work their magic on us in a pure way, as they did the storytellers.

Angel stories are proof of the Divine, proof that God has infinitely many hands with which to reach down into our mortal

lives and affect changes.

Angel stories are proof that we are always being noticed, that God and his angels are literally everywhere, all the time, assisting us. Our physical life is connected to a greater spiritual world beyond our comprehension; all the worlds connect through a bonding of love.

Angel stories are proof that God cares. And that when we say "Thank God," Someone says, *"You're welcome."*

A Passion for Angels

But why do I write about angels? In the beginning I didn't know the answer. I simply felt overwhelmingly compelled to think about angels, focus on them, and listen to what my own soul had to say. I was infatuated with the very idea of angels. I was falling in love.

The word "angel" lit up my soul, energized me—my whole being. I was supposed to think about angels, to look, listen, and hear. When I began, no one talked about angels. Yet, writing about them, I felt more understood by the presences that gave me the words to express my feelings than I ever had in my life.

The books I have written wrote themselves. I know the words are for everyone.

My angel adventure began over a decade ago, and since the angels "arrived," the universe has become an ongoing revelation to me. Now I realize I have always had angels and have even been aware of them to some degree, but only recently did I discover the right word for them.

The advent of angels in my life has been a miracle. They have been the surprise of my life and have, for me, made all the difference. But my excitement about these holy friends and my new light-filled life emerged from a deep need and a period of terrible darkness....

My Own Angel Story

The miracle and the trouble both began when I was born. The doctor was late, so my father caught me. He became my dearest angel. From that first moment my childhood was continuously filled with my father's angelic presence. A buoyancy and joyousness permeated everything.

As a child, I remember feeling the ecstatic presence of angelic beings—of joy and love all around me. I was not alone. In the air, in the sky, in blades of grass, in fingers of sunlight coming through my window, in the soft folds of my sheets and blankets, in my father's hug, in the wonder of colors and the feelings and sounds of music, in the essence of beauty, in the gentleness of love, even without a word for them yet, I knew angels.

My father's presence effortlessly bridged my happiest inner realms—my childhood heavens—with the realities of everyday living. A Harvard-trained psychoanalyst, yet remarkable in his plainness, Dad had a certain irrepressible light, a unique power and ability to love all people for exactly who they were and, always, to help you love yourself. My father made the world heaven for everyone around him.

I remember waking up very early in the mornings to shave beside him in the mirror standing on the toilet seat with shaving cream on my face, just like him, but using my razor without a blade. I loved going places with him. I loved the way he turned red when he laughed. I loved his big hands, the smell of his pillow in the morning. I loved his peacefulness and humor and

his depth in quiet times. I remember thinking how desperately I didn't want to miss anything. I couldn't bear the thought of missing a single moment of life. I never took him for granted. I never got used to him and never overlooked his specialness. My father was an angel. That is one thing I know. I never saw a boundary inside him.

Under his influence I flourished as an energetic, outgoing, optimistic kid with a dynamic family, friends, talents, and nerve. My dad was my unconditional support in everything I did. Like Lois Lane and Superman, I felt all I had to do was touch my Daddy's little finger and I could fly.

Suddenly, one Sunday morning, only two weeks before my thirteenth birthday, the terrible words "Your father's gone" hit me with the force of an atom bomb. He had had a massive heart attack. In one instant, a train hit me head-on. The walls fell down, the floor dropped out, the roof blew off, the sky caved in, and I exploded. I was alone…and for the first time I felt that reality was not safe. Instantly, everything stopped making sense. Life no longer felt like my friend. I was sure the light had gone out from the whole world. At twelve, I had no concept whatso-ever of death. The shock was an all-encompassing, devastating challenge for me. I shattered.

Though he was only thirty-nine years of age, thousands of people attended my father's funeral. Yet for the next twenty years no one spoke to me about this man. Not a word. I was never given a picture of him. I was never taken to his grave. We never had a family talk. My mother offered no solace. No one took over. No one counseled or even held me.

The dark, unanswered feelings that swelled in me from that

moment in my life became like a fever, a disease I eventually had to hide from the rest of the world. I had a few dreamlike years still under the lingering influence of my father's unconditional support and training, winning recognition, friends, and ribbons, before everything inside me collapsed. My family disintegrated. At the age of fifteen, I was sent away to private boarding schools, which only increased my loneliness and feelings of abandonment.

For many years I felt constantly that I was about to blow up. The riddle blazed endlessly throughout my consciousness. Is this a good universe or a cruel nightmare? Is God laughing at us? Are we absolutely meaningless? Is this all a big horrific, sadistic joke?

I expressed myself as best I could. Everywhere I went, in my own way I searched for answers and a solution to my misery—in three high schools, three colleges, my father's memory, his wisdom, in childhood dreams of movie stardom, and in the arts—dance, writing, art, music, drama, as well as philosophy, psychology, and finally spriritual seeking. But nothing helped.

During the next years I withstood an unrelenting feeling of being isolated from the world, continually appealing to the "greater forces that be" in private, demanding conversations with God, in the warmth of compassionate strangers, relationships with men, friends, drugs, alcohol, and then health food, self-improvement classes, and finally, meditation.

My writing teacher told me I was a writer, my dance teacher told me I was a dancer, my drama teacher told me I was an actress, but was life even worth living? I tried to hold on to my ambitions and my love of life, but everything could explode and disappear at any moment. Everything I loved could be ripped

away without warning. Senselessly. This I knew. My heart could be destroyed again, and I was certain I could not survive it.

I needed someone to put everything back together for me. I needed to fly again, but my father was gone, and there was no net now, no more magic. I had absolutely no sense whatsoever of my own future. For years I couldn't plan three days or three weeks in advance.

I moved seventeen times in ten years. My age changed, my addresses changed, my boyfriends changed, my appearance changed, but this didn't. I cringed in the shadow of my own failure to achieve, of intense family judgment—they had all gone on with their lives, but I was adrift, spiritually lost, emotionally starved, trying to function and fly but dying under the weight of my own self-condemnation and mistrust of the universe.

I tried in every way I could to live up to the ideals of my father, but I couldn't control the blackness that had crept over my soul. I felt that in my misery I had even betrayed my father's memory. I belonged nowhere and to no one. I didn't like being around people, I didn't like life or myself and certainly not God. I flung vacuous prayers into the universe with no idea if anyone was listening. The search for truth became my only ally.

I wasn't built for compromises. I felt God owed me a miracle or, at least, I knew I needed one. But even when I prayed it was to a God I no longer trusted. My need for answers became the angry center of my existence.

After college I moved to New York to continue my private quest for what I suppose I could call enlightenment. I worked for

the Sedona Institute, which taught the "Releasing" method, the best method I'd found to deal with my stress as well as to reach my goals. New York was an overwhelming environment for me most of the time, an ongoing confrontation with my own ambivalence about life. But it had its moments…bits of bright light kept poking through the harshness of New York, making me believe a miracle was possible.

One summer night I followed a crowd into a Simon and Garfunkel concert in Central Park. Uplifted and quite inspired in a crowd of half a million, I felt altered by the love and vulnerability in the two voices. When I got home, I sat down at my typewriter and wrote one sentence that changed my life forever. "Simon and Garfunkel are angels." That's all I wrote. The word **angel** suddenly lit up in Broadway neon in a flash of light inside me. It was as if I had never seen it before. A door opened in my heart and I heard music. I felt as if a spiritual bomb went off in my psyche and filled my head with fairy dust.

Angels. It was like remembering a tremendous secret, one I never should have forgotten. There was something gigantic in that word, something timeless, almost taboo in its purity, something utterly mysterious yet inherently important to my life. Angels were a key to something enormous. They were a piece of a sacred door to a forgotten part of my own soul.

I instantly became captivated, infatuated. I started writing angel sentences…angel thoughts. They came to me out of thin air. For weeks, I wrote about angels in taxicabs and elevators, in subways, coffee shops and walking down the street. Delightful little sentences spilled onto the pages of my notebook that answered profound questions, rang huge archetypal bells in my

consciousness, which had been silenced and repressed long ago. I laughed and I cried. They were magical words. They came from a different place than I was familiar with. They came from Heaven.

I experienced something stainless, deathless, and immediate in the thought of an angel that I'd never known anywhere else. My angel thoughts were a thread of light for me to follow. Still, I didn't know what to do with my angel writings. My angel realizations were incubating.

A couple of years and many little angel miracles later, in Los Angeles, feeling heartbroken from a recently ended relationship, I started visiting a certain chapel in the afternoons, to meditate. One day, having hit bottom yet again, I started deeply requesting guidance from the angels and the saints whose pictures lined the walls. To my blissful amazement, I asked questions and heard real answers…eloquent sentences…whole paragraphs, life-altering speeches flowing just for me.

As I became more receptive, I found these loving saints and angels right inside me, sitting next to my every thought, guiding all my feelings big and small. I laughed and cried with them, letting go of my old, hardened pain as never before, experiencing burst after inner burst of newfound, clean energy renewing me. I began to sit in this "releasing" process for several hours every day in their divine company. It was my favorite appointment. My job, I learned, was simply to be open. My trust grew and my sense of peace emerged. They reassured me that everything in my life would work out okay—in fact, beautifully.

Soon I felt continuously surrounded by angels and deeply loved. I knew my needs were finally, fully appreciated and I felt

quietly guided and infinitely befriended for the first time since my father's death. Over time, the damaged parts of me were lovingly gathered back into more of a working whole, guided by the angels' protective wisdom. All of a sudden my worries ceased, my insecurities ended, and soon, along with the completion of my first angel book, my life began to blossom.

Today I have an "angel career," and to my delight, the whole world is talking about angels. But when I began, no one mentioned them at all. I had to keep my interest in my invisible angelic companions and teachers a secret because people looked at me strangely when I told them about what I was doing. Nevertheless, many signs continually reminded me of the reality of my subject and my true connection to it. The angels have been very gracious.

When my first book was finished, I was "told" it would go all over the world. A year later I self-published a xeroxed copy and sold ten thousand books in ten months. I delivered every book by hand. Suddenly, three top publishers wanted it. My angel thoughts had become my career, and I discovered that many, many people felt about angels as I did.

Now I have a sense of safety and protection that extends beyond the boundaries of my activities and the activities of the world. I receive beautiful, magical letters. I am connecting with great numbers of people in a tender, spiritual way, and with the ongoing friendship of glorious angelic beings, I enjoy being alive in a more complete way than I've known before. My faith continues to grow. Everything the angels have told me has come true.

When I write about angels, I feel obedient and humble, uplifted and happy, moved and exposed. I feel a peace where

there is no sense of work at all. Today my books are published in ten countries and in seven languages. But mainly, I am happy. I am reassured constantly that my whole life is becoming an angel story in its own way.

Little by little the angels have brought me back out into the sunlight and surrounded my heart with the fresh air of living. My heart is alive now, because it knows it has angels. Angels don't die, you see. They can't be shocked away. You can't lose them as you can lose people. The deep answer to my dilemma was simple. Angels are eternal, and there is an "angelic soul" in each one of us. Angels never die; none of us really does. And should we ever doubt, worry, or wonder, angels are the proof.

For those whose lives have come to a terrifying halt at some point, angels are a good reason to come out of our shell. They protect us in ways that no one can see. They offer us their love, kindness, and safety when no one else understands what we need. When we can't put two and two together, when we can't define the trouble. Angels will help us fit back in when we've completely lost our footing. Angels will always take care of us. They will never go away.

Angels help us to remember that life never really comes to a screeching halt at all, no matter what the catastrophe, but continues in unseen ways. Despite what we can see, there is always the invisible...full of love, not frightened, never holding its breath for an instant. When we've had enough of trying to fight our battles on the material plane, we can always fall back on the invisible for comfort. Because no one ever loses friends in the invisible realms. Everything is always possible. No one ever dies. When you come to know angels, you understand that

nothing is ever lost. Not a moment, not a pin, not a feather, not a smile, not your self. And never, ever, an angel.

Mine is not really an unusual story. Out of necessity, I began to speak to saints and angels, and out of love, they began to speak to me. The grace I was offered was summed up in a word—**Angels.** It is a miraculous word. That word has become the seat of my existence and the soul of my life.

That is the word the angels offer to you....

The Sound of Encouragement

An angel's voice is never bitter or controlling. Never seductive or manipulative. Never a threat, never a bother. The angels know that you are in charge of your own life, that you control your own mind and have dominion over your world.

One day in Los Angeles, I walked into my room, locked my door, closed my windows, closed my curtains, and planted myself in the center of my bed. For weeks, I had been feeling an anxious fear about what I was doing in life. I had quit my sales job, was living off a car-accident settlement and was working hard, for many hours every day, exclusively on my first book. There were no other popular angel books at that time. I had never been published. People wondered if I was crazy doing this, so I didn't speak to many people. Though I felt tremendous happiness doing this work, I was at the end of my rope in terms of my anxiety about this issue. I decided I would sit

there…forever, if necessary, but something deep inside me insisted that I had to have a definite answer, a direct response from God, before I was willing to go on.

I focused inside myself as deeply as I could, speaking right to God, knowing it would take tremendous concentration to evoke a response. I figured I was up to it. That's how deep I perceived my need to be. Faithfully, I assumed that I was being heard by the omniscient, omnipotent, omnipresent ear, and with all the courage, will, and clarity I could muster, I poured my heart out. When I was finished, I waited. Soon I became very peaceful. Several minutes passed, and then I heard a loud sound from across the room. It was a familiar sound near my desk, like the rattle of my typewriter on the hollow wooden door that was my desk. But the typewriter wasn't plugged in. I thought, "What can that be? How can I be hearing that?"

I half believed I was imagining it. But then the sound came a second time and, a short while later, a third. I realized that the sound had come three times so that I would understand that it was, in fact, my answer. God had given me my own private miracle upon request, a sound of encouragement. And that was enough for me. I wondered why an ordinary sound had been the answer, but inside I knew that a miracle is a miracle, and God had answered.

I resumed my work on my book with new peace of mind. The funniest thing to me about this experience is that it wasn't until about three years later that I got the full benefit of this miracle. I was telling the story to someone, and that person said, "And Karen, isn't it wonderful, it was your *typewriter*!" I said, "What do you mean?" The miracle had involved the sound of

my typewriter, on which I was writing my first book. The answer had been, "Yes, you are going in the right direction, Karen.... Keep *typing!*" But I didn't even get the perfection of the joke. Not until much later.

The angels come together for our performing when we pay tribute through the gifts of music, dance, and art. When voices rise, they rise. When dancers leap, they leap. When melodies play, they play. When colors merge in joyful union, shape, and form, they do, too. They lead and follow, capture and free our strokes of artistic passion. The angels engage us in the art of love. And in art we are outdone by their magic until we engage them, and then we outdo ourselves.

The Footbridge

When we cherish each other, our angels adore us. When we surrender ourselves, they advise us. When we boast vainly, they wait for us to return to ourselves. When we feel helpless, they comfort us. When we feign weakness, they challenge us. When the world treats us coldly, they warm us with compassion. When we are all too frail and human, they protect us.

Once, meditating as usual in the little chapel, I had a vision of my father. It was not my imagination, because it was so real. I saw him just outside the building on the little footbridge in the sun, leaning over the rail looking at me and the swans. In my

mind, I went to him, and with his arm around me, we gazed at the swans together, just like in the old days. We loved swans. I had a long, long conversation with him that day. It soothed my soul no end. And then about a week later, sitting at my desk, I felt that my father was with me again. This time I got a lesson, a whole education in about an hour—complete with hugs and jokes as well as a deep, profound discussion about our unconditional relationship, his new wonderful home on the other side, the necessary reason for my long sense of aloneness, and my important job here. He was communicating how much he loved me, telling me he had received all my love as well. It was important for me to know not to grieve for him. He explained that he was surrounded by very loving beings, that his spiritual progress was continuing in a marvelous, rewarding way, and that we would always, always know each other. He affirmed all of my growth and let me know I was being carefully watched over. It was a most transforming encounter. It was very, very beautiful.

The sweetest, most innocent and trusting part of us will always find safety and understanding in the human angels who live here with us.

II

The Encounters
VISIONS

*T*o the angels, it is the undefended soul, the unguarded lover, and those willing to die for peace; the profoundly simple and the unashamedly pure, those content with little, the generous, and those always striving to be free; the hand-holding friend and the openhanded stranger, the impoverished, needy, humbled heart and the fully blessed one alike that are cause for Heaven's children to weep for joy....

Sometimes angels look human in form, but they are not. They enter our vision in forms we like, in disguises that appeal. Yet they don't frighten.

THE DENVER COP

I saw an angel. First time I ever told this story, I was kind of embarrassed to say so, but in retrospect, I really did. I'm a retired

Denver police officer, retired about four years. This happened back in 1971, when things were pretty turbulent out there on the streets.

We got a call to go out to a pretty rough area of town on a big disturbance, some kind of fight or something. At the time, we had just gotten those walkie-talkie units that you pulled out of the car, and that was the only communications we had.

When we got up to the scene, there was a pretty large crowd forming. This was early Saturday morning, and we wound up arresting a person. In the course of trying to put the struggling gentleman in the car, I set the walkie-talkie up on the roof. We finally managed to shove him into the backseat, my partner and I.

It was pretty busy that night. We didn't have any cover cars or anything, so we were kind of out on our own. The crowd was getting quite hostile, and before we knew it we were virtually surrounded. I went to grab the radio off the roof of the car, and it was gone. That was our only communications link. So we couldn't call for help or anything else. I was in a panic—like I said, it was a pretty rough crowd! It was one-thirty in the morning, and here my partner and I were cornered by this angry mob.

I glanced around at all the people there. Standing in the crowd was this little girl with blond hair—I can close my eyes and see her as if she's standing here right now. She looked like she was maybe four or five years old, which is really odd to think that she was even out at that hour of the night. She had on a white dress with little puffy sleeves. I don't know what the style would be called, but I remember the puffy little sleeves, all in pink trim and everything. She was just smiling at me, standing

42

there in little black patent-leather shoes. And she just kinda pointed over to the bushes.

Anyway, I went over, and to my amazement, I found the radio! Well, to make a long story short, I called for help, which finally arrived. And later on that day I told my partner, "Hey, if it wasn't for that little blond girl down there, I'd've never found the radio." And he said, "What little girl?" And I said, "The one in the little white dress!" And he said, "No way! I saw every person at the scene. There weren't any kids there!" So I figured it was an angel that pointed out the radio to me.

—AS TOLD TO THE AUTHOR IN A RADIO INTERVIEW

It doesn't matter if we are at the lowest level of civilization, primitive and wild, aging, ill, or newborn and raw with life, if we are average working Joes or leaders of great nations. Our relationship with angels is consistent with the thoughts in our minds and the receptivity of our hearts.

An angel story acts as an angel itself. It opens you; it puts you in touch with a deeper truth, a more divine reality. Angel stories remind you of unlimited compassion, worthiness, unshakable kindness, and infinite love.

❖   ❖   ❖

The rare and tender experiences of the meek, the gentle-hearted, and the persistently loving cannot be pirated by thieves

of the spirit like cynics, bigots, or tough intellectuals. To those fortunate people to whom Heaven bends an ear or whispers a promise, charts a course or bestows a revelation, reveals a vision, sends an apparition, or declares a mission, there are no longer juries, judges, or foes. There is only a bright light to follow and a song in the heart.

How does one prepare oneself for angels? Angels appear to the beautifully unprepared and the exquisitely ordinary. They appreciate an undistorted face, a nonjudgmental mind-set, a serviceful countenance, an unencumbered temperament.

THE FOSTER MOTHER

After I got saved and baptized in Jesus' name, I was living on West Bukthorn, and I'll never forget this. It was some years ago, and we were having these earthquakes. Remember when we had the big earthquake in '86? It was night. I was asleep, sleeping good, you know…me an' this baby. And something was saying, "Joanne, Joanne, get up! Get up!"

So I got up and I looked around. And the voice said, "Joanne, get up and sit on the edge of your bed." So I picked up the baby and we sat on the edge of the bed. And just as we sat down, an earthquake hit the house, BOOM! The windows over the bed shattered and the glass fell right where we had been sleeping. And I said, "Thank you, Jesus!"

Three days after that, I'm lying in bed and something woke me up—a bright light. I looked up and here's this great big, beautiful figure in the doorway. It was really pretty. It was a glowing figure, and I looked at it and I wasn't scared! You know, anytime you see something in your doorway, you're automatically going to jump and your heart's going to beat. My heart didn't beat, didn't do a thing. Because it was a peaceful-looking figure. It was just pretty. You know, really beautiful! It felt like my soul was being lifted out. My soul was just getting lifted up, and the only thing I could think of was Jesus, so I hollered, "Jesus!" And I felt myself come right back down into my body. That's when I looked to my door and this great big beautiful figure was there.

It was like God was talking to me and letting me know that

when I called Him, I was His. If it was a man or a woman, it didn't make a difference! I thought it was Jesus at first, because of the way it looked. It had this white on. I still believe it was Jesus, but everybody told me that it was an angel. I talked to a minister about it; it made me cry because it was so amazing, you know. I told my minister, "God visited me last night," but he said, "No, that was an angel. That was your protector. You are protected." All I know is that was the prettiest thing! I don't care what anybody says it was!

An' don't let anybody tell you that when you're walking with God, He doesn't let you know things. He sends a message to you. This voice was so clear for me. It was a woman's voice. "Joanne, get up!" An' then choo! It hit my house. That house just went *chchchchchchchch!* An' the windows broke. But nothing bad happened to me…that's because the Lord was with me.

Angels do come to you. They come in all kinds of forms and figures. And they're beautiful. Because that was pretty…that one spot in my door just lit up. I still think of it once in a while, you know, when I have problems or something. I call on God and I pray. I take care of a lot of children, you know.

I have plenty of faith in God and the angels…and the angels do come through this house. They have that beautiful glow. You know, it's like a glow of Life! People have to experience that. Like I said, every time I talk or think about it, even now, it brings tears to my eyes, because that was the most beautiful experience in my life. I know that God was with me from that day on.

Never be scared of an angel. You know why? I mean, if you've got faith in your heart, when a voice comes to you and tells you, "Do such and such a thing," that's the talk of the Lord. He just sent a message to you, and it could be in a man's voice or a woman's voice, but you get this little message. And then, when you do this, you'll see it comes out just the right way.

—JOANNE HERNANDEZ, INGLEWOOD, CALIFORNIA, FOSTER MOTHER OF SIX

Angels come and go quietly, invisibly, seamlessly, yet they are the most beautiful of all. They are irresistible, flawless beauties…male or female, clothed or unclothed, one hardly notices, they are so exquisite. They come dressed only in Spirit. We need no defenses. We have only an experience of their light, deep in our souls. We become so open, we hear, see, and feel only the message of love within this light. That is real, true beauty.

Their hands are prisms. Their heads are suns. Their hearts are roses. Their feet have feathers in them. Their shoulders hold oceanic souls in pain and joy. Their faces transfer ecstasy. Their thoughts are poems.

In a moment of connection we are thunderstruck by light! It beats on us and bathes us. It changes us, nourishes us, strips us…until we are light as well.

Angel stories teach us that nobody's special and we're all special. We do not have to be winning races to get the angels' attention or even to be out in the front of the pack. They appear

to the humble and the meek as well as to the courageous and strong.

❖ ❖ ❖

When Providence deems the time ripe to restore us to our Maker, or when for just a trifle or a little company we beckon their aid, they will fly tirelessly in our sphere, awaiting our call. And when they answer, their message floats into our ears in silence, surrounded by quietness.

The only desire the angels have is to gather us back into the essence of Heaven, the essence of love, our own happiness, at whatever moment we choose, whenever we decide we are ready to go Home.

THE HEAVENLY FLIGHT

I am a first-grade teacher at a Catholic school, and I had an angelic vision with my uncle that I will never forget until the day I die. He was diagnosed with prostate cancer, and I was very close to him. His nickname was Uncle Al, the Kiddies' Pal. I could never picture my life without him. He was like a second father to me. Visiting our house every Sunday when I was little, he brought toys and candy to me and my brother and sisters.

My uncle was in a lot of pain after surgery. The doctors told us he wasn't going to make it much longer. A couple of months thereafter, I had a vision at three in the morning in which I was standing in a hospital room holding on to plastic tubes. The tubes were empty—then I realized that they were in my uncle, and all of a sudden I heard him call my name. He used to call me Michie, for Michele. He said, "Michie, they want me to go up there," and he pointed through an opening in the ceiling into the sky. I said, "Where?" He said, "Up there!" He told me he was too afraid, and I said, "Uncle Al, what are you waiting for? That is Heaven. Come on, you don't have much time. You are so lucky. Let's go!"

I can't tell you what intense peacefulness I felt. All of a sudden, I took his hand and we floated up into the sky, over treetops, and we kept going higher and higher. It was as if all time had stopped. There were no worries, fears, or concerns about anything. We just drifted upward in a peaceful manner.

I was not allowed to look up, only straight ahead. My uncle released his hand from mine and floated upward, above me.

After a few seconds I was able to look up. I saw a hole in the sky with gold fluid pouring out. Then I saw this hole close up and the fluid went back into the hole. I floated downward and woke up in bed crying. My husband woke up and said, "Michele, what's the matter with you?" I told him that I was so upset because Uncle Al had died. He said, "No, he hasn't. We are going to see him tomorrow. Go back to sleep." I remember pointing at my husband, telling him that I knew that my uncle may not be dead right now but that he would die within the next few days.

My husband and I went to visit my uncle the next day. It was 7:00 P.M., and I called my grandmother from the hospital lobby to tell her we would be over for dinner later. She asked where I was calling from, and I told her I was on my way upstairs to see Uncle Al. She said, "Michele, he passed away ten minutes ago!" The doctor had just called the house. I hung up the phone and ran upstairs to his room. I was the first person to see him after he passed and I cried and held his hand.

I knew right then and there that I was blessed to be an angel to help my uncle to get to Heaven. I was sad to see him go, but an inner feeling told me that he was in Heaven with God now, in peace. His daughter arrived ten minutes later, crying. I told her all about my dream. She held on to me and said, "Michele, you really did help my father, because he was an atheist and he was so afraid to die. You helped him get to Heaven."

Through all the years I knew my uncle, I never knew he was an atheist. My uncle did know how much faith I had in God, so he came to me for help. It was a beautiful experience, and I no longer fear death. I know it will be peaceful. There are definitely a lot of angels in my life. I thank God every day for the blessings He gives me.

—MICHELE G. MALONE-SCARZELLA, BELVIDERE, NEW JERSEY, THIRD-GRADE TEACHER, HACKETTSTOWN, NEW JERSEY. SHE GIVES OUT "ANGEL POINTS" TO CHILDREN FOR WORK WELL DONE.

It is our job as human beings to learn about angels and love; to learn about death, separation, joy, peace. And no matter what anyone says to us, from what pulpit or platform, it is ultimately our task to open the door and to walk through that door ourselves, under our own steam, on our own terms. Only when we do that will we really know that we have been surrounded by angels all along, and we will know just how free we really are.

Our eyes may have seen all the wonders of the world, but to a soul in flight the experience of Heaven is more.

We mount the holy steps to freedom with wings aflame and hearts afire. The stars align above our heads in joyous surrender, with arrows bright toward the light. With wings outspread and hearts ablaze to Paradise and on we go, gathered up in wisdom, floating in love—seared through the heart, the mind, and the soul with truth.

Angels do not want to distract us from our lives, preferring

to be unseen friends, divine in purpose. And like any good friend, they stay out of our way and help us when they can.

CAUGHT BY AN ANGEL

About seventeen years ago I experienced the work of a life-saving angel. It was not for myself but for my four-year-old twin son, Kenny.

As I was busy working around a built-in pool, nine and a half feet deep, my son fell headfirst, backward, into the deep end of the cement pool drained of water. He got up without a scratch or a tear. I believe he was caught at the bottom before his head hit the cement. I have always believed he was saved by an angel.

Over the years my Kenny has been quite rambunctious. He has kept his angel awfully busy.

—BARBARA HEPBURN, WILLIAMSTOWN, VERMONT, ACCOUNTS-PAYABLE
CLERK, MOTHER OF ELEVEN

To be saved by Heaven we have to trust our angels, both human and divine.

THE RED BICYCLE

I had this dream about a bicycle when I was five. An angel appeared and said that I was going to get a bicycle. It was a little red bike. And I woke up the next morning, and there was the little red bike.

—ROBIN COVINO, LOS ANGELES, CALIFORNIA, ARTIST, HOUSEKEEPER

When we experience divine assistance, a fascination arises with the miraculous, the invisible, the perfect, and the free.

Angels do not look into our bank accounts, our résumés, or our medical reports to learn about us. They look into our hearts and our souls; and this is where we can always look to find them.

ANGEL IN THE NIGHT

---

*T*he most penetrating experience of mine happened back in the seventies in the middle of the night. I'm not sure what awakened me, possibly the brightness itself. I raised up in the bed, leaning back on my elbows, both amazed and frightened by this greatly illuminated form seeming to hover close to my chest. Drawing back, I called to my husband, who was lying next to me in a deep sleep.

My husband is one who admits to only what can be seen or

touched, and he is not the least bit curious about unexplained happenings. He's the type who will automatically respond with "It's nothing" if I should hear a strange noise.

But on this particular occasion, my husband gave me the satisfaction of at least knowing this was not my imagination. "What is it?" I asked. His answer came, fully alert. "I don't know," he said, "but it's bright enough!"

We were young then, and busy people, involved with the raising of children, keeping the household stable, attending the many affairs pertinent to a "normal" family environment. So busy, in fact, we shared little more than that common communication. It is not clear to me now how much time elapsed before the deep, penetrating, pure light disappeared. But it was quickly. I didn't fret over it. As a matter of fact, I drifted back into a restful sleep. I remember that my husband and I did discuss it briefly later, but probably not more than once; yet this was enough to validate the unusual manifestation.

It seems strange to me now, keeping the experience tucked inside. But the memory of this glorious light has never escaped me. Occasionally, I wonder what might have occurred had I not interrupted with the anxious calling of my husband's name.

During these past few years, since I began the habit of writing, I feel the presence of another form, variously peering over my shoulder, seeming almost to dictate or to point out passages that coincidentally fit into what I am working on.

—BETTY ANN WHITNEY, LAND O'LAKES, FLORIDA, REAL ESTATE AGENT, FREELANCE WRITER, AND ARTIST

The way to Heaven is not by death or separation, not by rebellion, but, rather, by love. When the soul reaches for that place beyond all striving, beyond all fear, beyond all unfulfilled longings and pain, like an angel it discovers the Infinite. And to accompany each of us on our flight, we are surrounded, nurtured, and adored by our angels.

Heaven opens its arms to us when we realize we have had enough of what we've previously known, when we want something entirely new yet inherently familiar, something that frees us and yet will never leave us, that makes us fully independent, yet finally united with the rest of the universe, full of wonder yet truly wise; unburdened, yet all filled up; completely loved and powerful yet deeply humble, surrendered, and at peace.

Angels speak our language. They understand our thinking and are able to work with us wherever we're at inside. They care about our welfare. They are truly "family," hidden only to the degree that we forget them. They are as much involved in your life as you are. Take a moment now and then to say hello to your angels and let them say hello to you.

Angels keep pace with Eternity and hover in the breezes of Paradise. They fly beyond our imaginations into our real selves.

MY LITTLE MUCHACHA

My first friend was a little Mexican girl I called Muchacha. I didn't know any Spanish at the time, but Muchacha and I spoke the same language, a child's language. Muchacha was what the big people called my imaginary friend.

I don't have many vivid memories of her, only that she was a constant friend and magical playmate. I came to realize in time that I was the only one who could see her. My mother couldn't see her. Muchacha explained to me that she was my special playmate, sent here only for me. I have always felt very blessed for her companionship.

As most adults who have had a childhood imaginary friend have done, I had for years chalked the memories of Muchacha off to childhood fantasy and normal creative development. However, one incident sticks out in my mind as one that was never explained. I remember being in a motel someplace, laughing at Muchacha because she was playing hide-and-seek with me from behind the curtains.

My mother and sister asked me what I was laughing at. I pointed over to the curtains and told them it was Muchacha and that she was playing hide-and-seek. I was nowhere near the curtains, nor was there any type of air vent nearby. But when my mother looked over, the curtain moved again, in plain view. I recall a look of curious confusion across her face—just for that moment, at least, she believed me.

As I have gotten older and read up on angel awareness and have formed true spiritual connections, I cannot help thinking

58

that Muchacha was my first true angel experience…. And perhaps my mother's, too.

—JENNIFER MILLWEE, VAN NUYS, CALIFORNIA, WORKS IN MARKETING
WITH SILICON GRAPHICS

Investigating angels is as natural as talking to yourself in the mirror about what bothers you and responding to yourself from a loving place. Angels are that close and that normal and that kind.

Childhood is a time when angels abound everywhere. There is hardly a thing or a person or a creature that is not an angel to a child.

In gestures of faith, we are never apart from our angels. In light, we reach them. In love, we become one with them.

We are moved, nourished, humanized, and enlightened in the angels' remarkable presence. We receive new information about who we are. We release false ideas. We are effortlessly changed by these encounters.

THE PRAYER

I haven't talked about this till the last couple of years, when I got angels back into my life again. When I was about eight years old, I was going to a Lutheran parochial school, and we did a lot of memorizing of Scriptures and prayers. It got to be so monotonous that I wasn't really paying attention. I was after the A in the class.

I remember one night in the wintertime, I went to bed, and I started to say the Lord's Prayer. I got about a third of the way through it, and I thought to myself, "What am I praying? What does this mean?" I kind of started to dissect the prayer, line by line, to figure out what I was actually saying. When I got to about the third line, I said to myself, "If there really is such a thing as God and angels, then show me...show me a miracle and prove it to me." We were at that point in school in the Bible where angels were showing themselves. So that was going through my mind—"If this could happen, then it could happen now; so if there really is something like this, prove it to me!"

I fell asleep that night, and in the middle of the night there was this light that was so bright in my bedroom that it woke me up. I remember sitting at the side of my bed, and my feet were on the wooden floor, and I remember it being very cold. I looked up and saw this huge angel by the stairway. And I thought to myself, "I wonder if I can take enough steps from my bed to where the stairway is, maybe I could touch an angel. I wonder if that would work." The angel was very tall, I mean, like eight or ten feet tall. It was looking at me and smiling. It was right there.

It had blond hair that shimmered like gold, in curls and waves. And as I got up close to it, I couldn't figure out if it was a man or a woman. It really didn't matter to me. It was wearing a long white gown, the typical angel that you see in pictures. And the whiteness of the gown and the wings was *so* white. I remember the wings were very thick. I could actually see every little feather that made up the wings. I just couldn't believe it. Every step that I took closer to the angel, the angel got a little bit lighter, almost like it was becoming more of a mist. And I took little steps…I didn't want to frighten the angel away. As I got up to the stairs, it just disappeared. When I talk about it, it still gives me goose bumps.

That night I didn't want to wake anybody up, so I went back to bed. But as I watched the angel, I remembered my grandmother used to say something about having to pinch yourself to know whether something is real or not. So I pinched myself really hard. In the morning when I woke up, I remembered seeing the angel and I remembered pinching myself. And when I looked, I had black-and-blue marks on my arms and legs where I had pinched myself to make sure that it wasn't a dream.

From that point on, I have never been able to recite a prayer that has already been written by someone else. As beautiful as the Lord's Prayer is and all the other prayers, I can never say a prayer that has been done by someone else. I always have to say it from my own heart.

I didn't really tell anybody about this because although my parents were churchgoers, I didn't really know if they believed in angels. Sometimes it is hard to believe when a younger person says something. We do that even today, I think. Anyway, I kept

it to myself. I absolutely did not tell my teachers or my friends. I didn't want them to think that I didn't believe, and I didn't want to stand out from anyone. I wanted just to stay in class and get my good grades, and I continued to memorize stuff. But it never meant anything to me anymore. Because I had more in my heart that I knew for a fact than anybody that was saying these things.

I knew an angel appeared to me and stood in my room on the night that I asked for a sign. I was never really the same after that. I would look around the class at school and wonder, "Do you really realize what you're saying? Does it mean anything?"

When I got older, I got married and had two sons. And I pushed the experience away from me. I really didn't take the time to have an angel in my life every day and acknowledge it and ask for help. Then I went through a really bad divorce. When I got to the lowest point probably in my entire life, and I had nowhere else to turn, I figured I might as well start praying again. When I was younger I really didn't need to pray, because I had parents taking care of me and I was okay. But now I am on my own and I am starting all over. And I know it is going to be a really hard road and I might as well ask somebody for help. And I directed my prayers to a higher being and my guardian angel. As soon as I started doing that, things started getting easier for me. I got to the point now that angels are around me all the time. I've gotten back into it.

I live in a two-story home in Simi Valley, and sometimes, because I am self-employed and I'm up a lot during the night working, I'll look out over the grassy area and I'll see angels out there. It isn't like it was when I was a kid and I saw the angel for the first time. This is more…almost like…almost like when you go to Disneyland. That's what it's like. Sometimes they come to me in my dreams. They come through a lot. They help me write songs. I have a lot of spirits around me; I have a lot of spirits surrounding my house. I'm really in tune to that.

—CAROL DONNELLY, SIMI VALLEY, CALIFORNIA, ENTREPRENEUR, ARTIST, SONGWRITER, FASHION DESIGNER, AND ACTRESS

They may appear as a human being, a dog, a bird, a puff of air, a gentle touch, a song on the radio, a dream, a vision of light, a child, a feathery, winged, haloed, immense glowing figure in a doorway, on a staircase, by the bed, or at the window.

When angels come into our hearts, in the deepest sense, the more useful they become and the more profoundly they affect us. Angels are a key provided for our enlightenment.

When you practice opening to angels, it becomes effortless, as instantaneous as changing your thought, shifting your point of view, opening a certain window in yourself and looking through it, moving your attention to a happy place.

THE LITTLE ANGEL IN WHITE

I did have an experience about a year and a half ago. I believe I saw an angel. My boyfriend and I were sleeping. I woke up in the middle of the night, looked at the end of the bed, and saw what appeared to be a white little person, almost like a child. I was not dreaming, because I sat up and screamed. My boyfriend asked me what was wrong, and I told him a little white angel was at the end of the bed. I saw it only for a matter of seconds. Although I did scream very loudly, I was not scared, just shocked.

My boyfriend kind of laughed, but I can still vividly remember how this angel was sitting and looking. I believe in God and angels. And no, I am not crazy. I am a pretty conservative person who grew up in a very Catholic family.

Also, a couple of years ago, my boyfriend and I went skiing. The mountains and view looked so pretty that I took a picture. When it was developed, I couldn't believe it. It is a picture with a figure of light—of an angel with open arms. It's the most amazing thing. It's so visual.

A couple of my friends say, "Oh, it's the light, or the camera, or something." It's not. It's a picture. I usually keep it in my Bible. I have it here at work in my desk.

—NAME WITHHELD

The more we open to angels, the more spiritual rewards and blessings we will receive. Everything will change—our thinking, our perceptions, our feelings, and the way we conduct ourselves, even the way others treat us.

❖   ❖   ❖

To find the world of angels we must be bold even as children are, and fearless like birds who dive into the sea, and trusting like wheat that waves in the wind, surrendering.

FALLING OUT OF BED

Mine was a very simple, visual encounter with my guardian angel. I was five years old and I fell out of bed. I actually saw my angel try to catch me. He was definitely male, with curly, light brown hair. He had wings and a flowing robe. He was at the foot of my bed, and he dove to catch me. That was thirty-seven years ago, and I can still see him plain as day.

He is a very patient angel, as I always tried to slam him in the cellar door after running up the stairs real fast. And I also would sit down in a chair real hard and try to squish him!

—SUE MONAHAN, WINTER PARK, COLORADO, CLEANING LADY,
WATERCOLOR ARTIST

Only the secret heart, the most simple inner friend, truly knows what life is about, and loves it.

For every event here below, the angels gather. For every trip and fall, for every leap into divine passion, for every crucifixion or rise to glory of the human soul, they gather silently. In twos and threes, in flocks like flowers in a breeze, the angels ride the length and breadth of human frailty—sending love.

To angels, there are no favorites. We all have equal opportunities to be chosen, to be loved, to be happy. In fact, they say it is we who are choosing in our hearts in every moment.

To be with the angels . . . it is not quite enough to trust just a little. One must trust completely, like a tiny child . . . to fly.

THE GLOWING FIGURE

Well, I was in fourth grade, about eight or nine years old. I'll never forget—my mother and father had been separated for a while and it was Christmastime. So I lay down under the Christmas tree and I was watching *Cabin in the Sky* on TV. It's really a good movie, and I'll never forget looking at it that night. It must have done something to me, because I felt high. I had a little twin bed at the end of my mother's bed, a sofa that folded down, because we had only a one-bedroom apartment. I'll never forget that when I went to get into bed, there was this glowing white object lying in my bed. I didn't do anything. I just kneeled down and said my prayers.

I wasn't scared. I felt good. I felt warm and good inside, and I was happy. I said I hoped my mother and my father would get back together—you know, like most kids that age. Then I got into bed, on the edge of the bed, and I said, "You can have my pillow." It was the figure of a person. It looked like an angel with wings folded up lying there. That's what it looked like. And it was glowing. That's why I wasn't scared.

Picture me; I am on the edge of the bed almost falling over on the floor. About four o'clock that morning my mother wakes up and says, "Boy, what are you doing? Why don't you get in the bed right?" And I said, "Nope, my angel is sleeping beside me." And she said, "What do you mean? Get up." I got up and I showed her that my pillow had an indentation in it. Someone had been lying there. My mother looked surprised. "You didn't slip off?" she said. And I said, "No, I've been sleeping on the edge of the bed. I gave my pillow to my angel. I told her she

67

could have my pillow, and that's who was sleeping there." And my mother jumped to the phone and called my grandmother.

I told my grandmother. My mother said the covers had been folded back from the other end and my pillow had an indentation like somebody's head had been lying there. And my mother said to me, "That was your guardian angel." And I said, "Yeah." And I told her, "I prayed that you and my dad would get back together and everything would be all right for us. And when I got into bed, my angel was lying in the bed, and I just told her, 'It's okay. I'll just sleep on the side.'"

The experience made me an individualist. I felt it was a message. My mother would get on my case because I used to run with this one little guy down the street and if he said, "Do this," I did it. After that I had nothing to do with what he said. After this experience I became more mature. I would have gotten in trouble. I think I would have ended up a follower. This guy I followed—to this day he's on drugs. He's been in jail two or three times. And the clan I used to run around with just got killed a few years ago, robbing someone. That was the area we had to live in because we couldn't afford to live anyplace else. I know a lot of things have happened to me where I came out okay that are pretty miraculous.

Since then, I live and let live, I don't drink, I never got high, and I've never smoked in my life. I think that little incident that happened to me just changed me. I would have ended up a follower. I know it. I think that that angel did a lot to change my life.

Maybe they knew that my father and mother would never get back together. Maybe the angel visited me just to make me strong. And then my father got killed in a car accident when I was twelve. So I helped my mother with my sisters. They grew up healthy and

strong, too. And so have all my own children; no drugs, no big problems. I've always been successful in everything I tried. I think seeing that angel in my life was a great blessing. It made me live for myself, live and let live, not get involved in trivialities.

I have some friends who say, "Oh, man, I don't believe in that mess. Why don't you get off that, man?" And I look at their lives and their lives are total chaos.

My feeling is that angels come to you if you believe. You have to believe. It will help you. I think they're there to protect you and guide you from your mishaps, because I know, if she hadn't come to me, I would've gone a bad way.

—DORSEY DOUGLAS, LOS ANGELES, CALIFORNIA, *PROFESSIONAL MUSICIAN WITH A GOLD RECORD, SUCCESSFUL BUSINESSMAN, AND FATHER*

It is a happy thing to know an angel. It is without cast of doubt or suspicion—without traces of cloudy thinking or unkempt thoughts. It is joy like the center of an embrace, like the thought of pure love, like the inside of a cloud shot through with golden rays of light.

To these great souls in children's pose the angels cling and hover, to these sincere lovers who request angels' love in tender, unclothed voices, who uninhibitedly tread the path with rough, torn feet because they know it is the only path that goes the distance.

To these uncluttered ones, the angels send their messages of redemption; they caress with wise admissions of favor, they wash

off the scabs of life's great woundings and pour fresh elixir of joy about their path. To these the angels sing and answer, to these the angels come.

Surrounded by Your goodness, illuminated with Your light, let me feel the blessings of Your loving power running through me. Make this day special and sacred and devoted to You. Let me be Your little one, full of Your grace, filled with Your kindness and a friend to everyone I meet. Let me know the bliss of Your presence and the heart of Your understanding.

THE PREGNANT MESSAGE

I am thirteen years old and would like to tell you my own angel story. My parents were living in South Carolina before I was born, far away from my grandparents in Virginia. Mom and Dad were more than a little afraid that the birth of their first child would happen without any family around. They felt alone and wondered if they would recognize the first signs of labor.

Very early one morning in August, my mother had a special experience. Just before she was fully awake, the figure of a woman dressed in a white gown suddenly appeared to her, interrupting the dream she was having. My mother somehow understood that her dream had ended because something very special was unfolding. She was not afraid of the figure but felt very calm in her presence. She said the woman communicated to her that her name was Katherine.

But all the woman said was, "Happy Birthday!" My mom became confused and said, "But my birthday is in January." The woman said, "You are not listening to what I have said, Happy BIRTH-day." The woman then vanished. At that very second, my mom's labor started, and then she understood the message; today would be the birth-day of her child. My mom had feared she would not know when labor would begin, but here was an angel calming her and telling her the one thing she wanted to know more than anything. My name is Katheryn in honor of this very special angel.

—ERIN KATHERYN GOODIN, FAIRFAX STATION, VIRGINIA,
A FRESHMAN AT PAUL VI HIGH SCHOOL

Our angels hear us though we speak so softly of what we love. They approve of us though warring armies battle within our fear-crazed personalities. Angels know us more fully than we know ourselves on happiest days and love us more perfectly than we have ever loved at all.

Some say the angels keep to themselves and only watch us from behind a veil of invisibility, but this is only half true. The angels are ever within and around us, just as we are ever within and a part of God.

To the angels all mysteries end in love.

could have my pillow, and that's who was sleeping there." And my mother jumped to the phone and called my grandmother.

I told my grandmother. My mother said the covers had been folded back from the other end and my pillow had an indentation like somebody's head had been lying there. And my mother said to me, "That was your guardian angel." And I said, "Yeah." And I told her, "I prayed that you and my dad would get back together and everything would be all right for us. And when I got into bed, my angel was lying in the bed, and I just told her, 'It's okay. I'll just sleep on the side.'"

The experience made me an individualist. I felt it was a message. My mother would get on my case because I used to run with this one little guy down the street and if he said, "Do this," I did it. After that I had nothing to do with what he said. After this experience I became more mature. I would have gotten in trouble. I think I would have ended up a follower. This guy I followed—to this day he's on drugs. He's been in jail two or three times. And the clan I used to run around with just got killed a few years ago, robbing someone. That was the area we had to live in because we couldn't afford to live anyplace else. I know a lot of things have happened to me where I came out okay that are pretty miraculous.

Since then, I live and let live, I don't drink, I never got high, and I've never smoked in my life. I think that little incident that happened to me just changed me. I would have ended up a follower. I know it. I think that that angel did a lot to change my life.

Maybe they knew that my father and mother would never get back together. Maybe the angel visited me just to make me strong. And then my father got killed in a car accident when I was twelve. So I helped my mother with my sisters. They grew up healthy and

69

strong, too. And so have all my own children; no drugs, no big problems. I've always been successful in everything I tried. I think seeing that angel in my life was a great blessing. It made me live for myself, live and let live, not get involved in trivialities.

I have some friends who say, "Oh, man, I don't believe in that mess. Why don't you get off that, man?" And I look at their lives and their lives are total chaos.

My feeling is that angels come to you if you believe. You have to believe. It will help you. I think they're there to protect you and guide you from your mishaps, because I know, if she hadn't come to me, I would've gone a bad way.

—DORSEY DOUGLAS, LOS ANGELES, CALIFORNIA, PROFESSIONAL MUSICIAN WITH A GOLD RECORD, SUCCESSFUL BUSINESSMAN, AND FATHER

It is a happy thing to know an angel. It is without cast of doubt or suspicion—without traces of cloudy thinking or unkempt thoughts. It is joy like the center of an embrace, like the thought of pure love, like the inside of a cloud shot through with golden rays of light.

To these great souls in children's pose the angels cling and hover, to these sincere lovers who request angels' love in tender, unclothed voices, who uninhibitedly tread the path with rough, torn feet because they know it is the only path that goes the distance.

To these uncluttered ones, the angels send their messages of redemption; they caress with wise admissions of favor, they wash

off the scabs of life's great woundings and pour fresh elixir of joy about their path. To these the angels sing and answer, to these the angels come.

Surrounded by Your goodness, illuminated with Your light, let me feel the blessings of Your loving power running through me. Make this day special and sacred and devoted to You. Let me be Your little one, full of Your grace, filled with Your kindness and a friend to everyone I meet. Let me know the bliss of Your presence and the heart of Your understanding.

THE PREGNANT MESSAGE

I am thirteen years old and would like to tell you my own angel story. My parents were living in South Carolina before I was born, far away from my grandparents in Virginia. Mom and Dad were more than a little afraid that the birth of their first child would happen without any family around. They felt alone and wondered if they would recognize the first signs of labor.

Very early one morning in August, my mother had a special experience. Just before she was fully awake, the figure of a woman dressed in a white gown suddenly appeared to her, interrupting the dream she was having. My mother somehow understood that her dream had ended because something very special was unfolding. She was not afraid of the figure but felt very calm in her presence. She said the woman communicated to her that her name was Katherine.

But all the woman said was, "Happy Birthday!" My mom became confused and said, "But my birthday is in January." The woman said, "You are not listening to what I have said, Happy BIRTH-day." The woman then vanished. At that very second, my mom's labor started, and then she understood the message; today would be the birth-day of her child. My mom had feared she would not know when labor would begin, but here was an angel calming her and telling her the one thing she wanted to know more than anything. My name is Katheryn in honor of this very special angel.

—ERIN KATHERYN GOODIN, FAIRFAX STATION, VIRGINIA,
A FRESHMAN AT PAUL VI HIGH SCHOOL

Our angels hear us though we speak so softly of what we love. They approve of us though warring armies battle within our fear-crazed personalities. Angels know us more fully than we know ourselves on happiest days and love us more perfectly than we have ever loved at all.

Some say the angels keep to themselves and only watch us from behind a veil of invisibility, but this is only half true. The angels are ever within and around us, just as we are ever within and a part of God.

To the angels all mysteries end in love.

D.J. AND THE THREE ANGELS

I saw a mean little spirit that was on this wall right here. It had a horse coming out from the side. It wasn't scary, but it was mean. He turned around and he made us an ugly face. Then I said, "Gran'ma, wake up!" She said, "Go back to bed. God will chase 'em away. They're not in here no more."

So I went back to my room, and all I saw were three little angels. They had wings coming out from their thighs, and they were all standin' there, smilin', laughin', and their wings went like this [he cupped his hands and then opened and closed them like wings]....They changed to white; then they went back to gray. The mean little spirits, then...they just left.

I like angels. I feel safe when they're around. I think they're around all the time, even when I'm at school, because there are a lot of bullies up there at school. They do stuff, and I just walk away, knowing that there are angels that take care of me.

—D. J. COLLARD, INGLEWOOD, CALIFORNIA, EIGHT YEARS OLD

We cannot keep from angels' blessings. It is impossible.

The angels' kindness and mercy bend to every hopeful wish for happiness, every trusting thought of love, every decision to bare one's soul, every effort to be loving, and every lasting vow of goodwill whether whispered in silence or aloud.

73

Angels come from a holy reality just beyond our awareness and always lead us to that place just beyond our vision where our true home and happiness are.

The angels cannot change our minds but only affirm what we already know at a deep level. The more deeply we accept their presence, the deeper affirmation we are able to receive.

We can approach our angels through prayer, meditation, devotion, selfless action, releasing false desires, surrender to higher wisdom and love, and finally by grace.

It is the angels' duty to surround sweetness and virtue, to stalk perfection.

THE ANGEL ON THE PORCH STAIR

I'm eighty-two, and I received my First Communion when I was about thirteen. I was such a holy girl that day—I kept saying to myself, "If I died today, I could be an angel!" I was so thrilled to have a veil on my head. I was really holy....

My brother and I got home from church, and then we had to go to school. We walked about two miles a day back and forth because in 1926 there weren't too many cars. So this special day, we'd come home, had breakfast, and then gone to school. That night at seven we had to go in for our scapulars. It's like an image of the Sacred Heart, a religious garment you put around

your neck, one piece in the front and the other on the back. They had a benediction for about five hundred kids who were receiving that day. It was a big church!

We must have gotten out of church about nine o'clock. My brother and I were walking home alone. We tried to run, but we had to go through fields and all. It was very hard. It started to rain pretty good, so we got home about ten o'clock, and by the time I undressed it was late.

My father was a miner. He and my mother were already in bed. My mother kept chickens and ducks and cows and lots of animals. She was an animal lover. We all went to bed real early because we all had our chores to do every day. We didn't get to play like the other kids. Our parents were both pretty strict. So this night, my father and my mother were already asleep.

Before I got into bed, I had to use the john. We had no bathroom in the house. There was no plumbing anywhere in that area. We had a huge grapevine growing from our porch all the way to where our outlet was…a huge grapevine, and my father had it fixed so pretty that you could sit under it. It was real shady; it was really very nice.

I had to use the bathroom, so I started to walk down our steps from the porch; we had about seven or eight steps. I got to about the middle and…oooh! A terrible gush of wind came through! It was really powerful! And in that wind flew a white dove, a white bird. It didn't frighten me, because I thought it was one of our pigeons just coming in. We had lots of pigeons, but that bird got up so high, then turned right around and flew over our grapevine. Then it got under the grapevine. It was floating, floating down. It was sort of leaping down. It was

75

coming toward me, and it was so *beautiful*.

Well, before this bird reached the ground, it turned into an angel! It was just beautiful! She was a large person, a full figure. I'm five foot three, and she was every bit my build. She wore a blue gown and she had a light around her head. I saw she had a crown on her head with a star as she was floating down. That star was just like a beam of light. And her gown was all blue; she had a gold sash tied around her waist hanging down, and her wings were open, but not quite open, just nice. She was floating down, barefoot. She was almost at about the second step, and I just started screaming! I said to myself, "I *said I wanted to be an angel—but I'm too afraid to become one right now!*"

I could hardly open the door fast enough. I really thought it was going to take me. I didn't even look back when I started screaming. I just couldn't find the door fast enough to get in! I was truly scared to death! I started screaming, and my father and mother jumped up out of bed. They wanted to know what was wrong. I told them an angel had come for me, and my mother said, "Well, what did you start screaming for?" And I said, "You'd scream, too, if it was coming for *you!*" My mother believed me. I guess my mother is a believer. After that I was thinking I shouldn't have been afraid. Maybe the angel had something good to tell me.

The next day at school, I went up to the sister and told her that I saw my guardian angel! The sister had glasses, and her eyes were peering at me over the top of her glasses. She said to me, "What?" I told her the story. She said, "Well, Helen, we are much holier than you and we have never seen anything like that!" "Well," I said to her, "I'm telling you the truth! I did! An' I'll tell you how it looked! It was *gorgeous!*"

I always used to pray to my guardian angel when I was a girl, so I think that's why she came, I guess. I still pray to her. She was so beautiful….

—HELEN OSOLINICK, SCOTTSDALE, ARIZONA

Fear alone may block the angels from getting too close to us…or at least from our perceiving their nearness. Doubt blocks angels who are trying to communicate with us.

Accept the possibility of an apparition or a miracle; eradicate fear and mistrust of heavenly meetings and gestures from your heart and mind. If we can't trust angels, whom can we trust?

❖ ❖ ❖

Sometimes it takes ropes and ladders and rescue teams; small inching maneuvers; one toehold, then another, one groping hand to find a fingerhold and then another. That is faith.

CROWN OF STARS

When I was small, age ten, an angel came to me dressed in blue, wearing a wreath of flowers upon her head. She spoke to me without moving her lips and said, "It will be difficult, but do not worry, it will be all right." Shortly after, I had an illness that

crippled me for six weeks. It was bad. It has been difficult in my life, but all right. I have never forgotten the lovely angel.

—A. Friend, Long Beach, California, counselor

Angels don't owe us a miracle to convince us of their reality. But when we are simply receptive, they like to give us one.

❖ ❖ ❖

Children can see everything as it is in Heaven. They see everything as filled with light. They notice that adults do not, and the difference disturbs them very much.

The angels are making themselves known to us all in a natural way—to let us know we're not alone. To give us faith. To remind us of the right direction to go in and that Heaven is real.

For in the unlocked heart, nowhere do the angels see any wall to keep Heaven out, or the presence of an enemy…only open souls, willing, honest, and magnificent.

THE DANCING APPARITION

My younger brother is nine years old. Two years ago his classmate's mother was in the kitchen cooking up a meal. And her son came in (he would have been about seven), and he said, "Mom, there's a woman in your room dancing on your bed and dancing around the room." And the mother said, "What are you taking about?!" She walked with him into her bedroom and saw the apparition. They were standing there together, just looking at it, and she was very scared. She screamed, "Get out of here, what do you want?" The apparition stopped. The mother started ranting and raving ordering this vision to go away. And the son just said, "Mom, it's okay. She says don't be scared of her." So then the mother stopped yelling and turned to her son. "How do you know that? What does she want? Ask her what she wants!" He did. The boy said, "Well, she just wants to let you know that she's my guardian angel!"

—MONICA MARIE DOWNER, LOS ANGELES, CALIFORNIA, TELEVISION
WRITER, RESEARCHER, AND ASSOCIATE PRODUCER FOR ASSOCIATED
TELEVISION IN LOS ANGELES

Is it really silly, unrealistic, or childish to believe that angels exist? Perhaps if we relinquish our sarcasm, mistrust, and doubt, and pay attention with innocence in our hearts, we will receive instruction from Heaven. For that is all Heaven wants—just a little attention.

Today, the media are spreading news of violence like a firestorm…advertising it, focusing on it millions of times a day all around the world…making it a part of our thinking, our normal vision of life. The children are getting a terrible message.

Children need to be taught about angels, about heavenly subjects. This world is not enough. There are no answers or explanations here for the things that upset us.

Children feel the ecstatic presence of loving beings that surround them, frequently, if not always. They attract the angelic part of our personalities, too, since they are still "a little bit closer to Heaven" themselves. It is the awareness of the abundance of pure joy available to all of us that makes a child's heart so resilient yet so sensitive to pain and why a child's tears are so poignant. Their awareness of divine joy is also why children feel such disappointment when we're not all happy, when we don't all love one another, when we can't see happiness, see miracles…because they do.

Angels encourage us to scale the walls of circumstance, to swim the ocean of confusion, and blast across the vacuum of resistance straight into the heart.

❖　❖　❖

Of angels, wise men have said, they reflect the stars in their brightness, the moon in their mellowness, the sun in their sweetness, and the heart in its fire.

In faith we ascend the earthly stair to the Divine One, our passions dissolving, our energies uniting. We cannot bear to think a thought apart…and so soar upward.

HEAVENLY RECRUITERS

A little over eleven years ago I had an encounter with four angels. I will never forget this for as long as I live. The experience I had haunts me to this day. I always thought that angels were beings of love, peace, joy and security...until I saw these beings face-to-face.

One night, I got angry at God because I blamed Him for all the things that were going wrong in my life. I cursed up at the stars and shook my fist at the sky. That same night I had a dream I was joining the army in Louisville, Kentucky, and angels were the recruiters sorting us out. They wore long white robes, they were very tall, probably ten feet. They had wings that came out of their shoulder blades and almost touched the floor. The wings are what frightened me the most. The recruits that didn't fit the bill were put in a separate room away from the chosen recruits. I was put in the room with the rejects. This frightened me so much that I ran out of the room in search of the angels so I could try to convince them I could make a good soldier, but they were already gone.

All I found was a man all alone, of normal size, wearing only a white cloth across his midsection. I asked him to let me join the "chosen" people. He averted his eyes from me, and I woke up.

As I opened my eyes and saw my room as it has always been, there at the foot of my bed was this angel of normal size and had no wings. We kept our eyes on each other, and he slowly started floating off the floor and went right through my ceiling.

—WILLIAM M. JONES, PINE KNOT, KENTUCKY, LANDSCAPER

Angels sometimes make our consciences speak loudly when we're wrong. Yet self-condemnation is very difficult for the angels to get through because it is opaque. It is a negative retreat in the dark where angels are not allowed.

Angels appear to prove the boundlessness of love and the unlimited power that transcends our world.

Don't force yourself to believe in angels. Let go of the disbelief and find them everywhere.

In truth we are all much closer than we have ever imagined. Our hearts are a part of one another not only here but on the other side, too. We are blessed forever by the many friends we have. We can never be alone and never have been. Friendships of all kinds are merely an affirmation of what we are.

THE PICTURE

When I was in college at Berkeley, I was a rower. I rowed thirty hours a week. I'd wake up at five in the morning, work out at five forty-five or six o'clock for several hours, and I was a student all day. I worked in the afternoons from three to six. By nine o'clock, you can imagine, I was dead tired. And in an hour I would normally be deeply asleep.

This particular day, I'd gone to sleep about ten. At eleven, I suddenly woke up, fully awake, and saw my friend Greg. But the summer before, Greg had killed himself.

He was just standing there in the middle of the room, pointing behind me. I immediately turned, and I caught a heavy, framed picture in midair as it fell off the wall. If I had been lying in my bed asleep it would have fallen directly on my head and the glass would have shattered all over me.

Greg was one of my closest, oldest, and dearest friends, kind of like my first love as a child, when I was five. We had grown up together. His younger sister was my best friend. And my brother was his best friend. We all missed him terribly.

So after I caught the picture, I looked back and he was gone. But I felt he became my angel—one of my angels. I'm a lucid dreamer. Ever since I was a child, I've had very vivid dreams. Every day I'd come down and I'd be like the breakfast entertainment. You know, I'd just tell my dreams. And since Greg died, he comes into my dreams, he'll come into my dream and sit down and watch or hang out or chat, you know. . . . He just makes himself known.

—Monica Marie Downer, Los Angeles, California,
TELEVISION PRODUCER

When we know angels, we are so amazed with life, we cannot be afraid of death...and all our stories end in blessings.

Rescues

Sometimes we like taking credit for the behavior of our universe, and at other times we can't explain our lives at all.

The Car with a Mind of Its Own

In 1987 I had a nearly new car, a BMW, my very first BMW, and I was in love with it. I had a little talk with it one night in the garage sitting in it in the dark, promising it that I would always take care of it. I would always wax it when it needed waxing, buy it new shoes, and keep it cared for and clean. And in return, I wanted it to care for me, too. I wanted it to start whenever I needed to get somewhere and I wanted it to be safe on slick roads. I had this really neat agreement with my car and then never thought about it again; just released it and let it go.

About a year after that, I was driving toward a really busy, wide intersection. I was far enough away that I could tell the light was going to change, so there was no point in slowing down, putting on my brakes. And there was nobody in front of me, so I just continued going at the same speed. I could see I already had a green light when all the power in my car stopped! The radio went off, the power steering was gone; but instead of the normal momentum of a big, heavy car, the car almost

instantly came to a stop, but without a jerk; like real soft hands had held it from going forward!

I looked down at all the gauges to see if anything was lit up because I had no idea what could be wrong. Nothing was on at all, and I looked back up just in time to see a car going across the intersection about ninety miles an hour, with two police cars right behind it, at exactly the *same moment* I would have been there. All three of them would have broadsided me!

The minute that the second police car cleared the intersection, all the power came back on in my car—every bit, everything! The radio came back on, the air conditioning continued to blow, the car continued to move, and I never put my foot on the gas again, either. I didn't even *touch* the gas. The car just started going again.

As soon as I got through that intersection and I was safe on the other side, on the shoulder of the highway, I pulled off because I was shaking quite a bit. And I really just wanted to be thankful. I wanted just to sit still and thank God and get myself collected. Then a little wing started brushing against the side of my face. It felt just like feathers on the side of my face. I couldn't see anything, but it brushed against me for two or three minutes while I kept thanking God for protecting me from what probably would have been a deadly accident. I don't know how I could have survived.

I will never forget looking up from the dashboard and seeing those cars going through that intersection. And I mean they were going so fast, people were scattering to get out of the way. And other cars were scattering to get out of the way, and I would have been right in the middle of that at that time, and at the

speed I was traveling—forty miles per hour—we would have been perpendicular to each other right in the center. Those two police cars couldn't have stopped in time. It would have been all four of us—one big pile. It was *really* amazing.

That was my very first experience. When the angel came the first time and brushed against me over and over again, I said, "Is that my angel that I have talked to so long?" It brushed again really quick, as though it were answering me. It was really important to me. It was the most vivid demonstration of that power that's within us all the time to protect us. I guess I was just in a mode of total trust and it just worked through me without my blocking it.

Since that point, my angel comes back the same way by brushing its wings against my cheek. There's never been anything else that dramatic, but many, many minor things have happened as if to say, "Don't go that way or don't do this or don't touch that." Oh, it really protects me very, very vividly. I mean it's not questionable. I know when it's there.

—Nancy Spencer, Chesterfield, Missouri, housewife

Angel experiences may sometimes confuse or dramatically soothe us, shake us up or calm us down; they change our perceptions, straighten out our thinking, yet blow our minds.

Angels hide radiantly, within every beautiful moment,

chanting the name of Heaven within the leaves and droplets of water, singing in the new grass and thundering in the sky.

In a sense, we control our own lives, but in an equally true sense, we can never fully control anything. We don't even know how we arrived at this experience called Life or where we go when we leave it. There are invisible forces behind everything.

In the world of angels, every day is a day for love and good luck falls on all well-opened travelers.

THE SAILBOAT

In June 1981, after I'd been here in Houston a couple of years, an old boyfriend called and asked if I wanted to go out sailing with him. I said, "I'll always go sailing." We drove down to his brand-new thirty-foot sailboat, which was in a slip near Galveston. We departed from a big cove, crossing the Houston ship channel, which is a deep trough, a kind of shipping lane that goes all the way from the ocean up through Galveston and way, way inland to Houston. We had to sail way out before we hit the open water. You are out on this big bay and there'll be great big ships coming along, commercial ships.

It was Saturday morning; we'd been out a couple of hours when my friend dropped anchor. He wanted to take some pictures. He said, "Just hang on to the steering wheel. Don't steer or anything. Just aim straight ahead and make sure that you

always see that point in front of you." After a while he said, "Well, let's get out of here." And he started changing the sails.

The boat began to turn around, and suddenly, there we were, just seconds away from an oncoming huge barge that was about two city blocks long. I had seen this thing maybe fifteen minutes or half an hour before, and it was far away, moving in another direction. But now it had veered around and was coming right at us.

I said, "George, what do we do now?!" He said, "There's nothing we *can* do." It was still coming. I was standing in the stairs, going down to the galley. And I put both hands up on the sides of the door frame. I said, "Nothing bad has ever happened to me before and it's not going to now!" And boom! The barge hit the boat. I didn't see my boyfriend. He told me later that he dove off the side. I just stood frozen still, saying, "It's not going to hit. It's not going to hit."

Well, I fell back inside the galley. And what happened is, the whole barge went right over the sailboat with me in it. I was inside the galley with bedsheets swimming around me, getting caught around my neck. And the date flashed before my eyes: June 20, 1981. I thought, "Oh! So that's the way it's going to be. This is the way. This is the day." I thought, "Well, just take a breath of water and it'll all be over." But, you know, your psyche won't let you do that. I said, "You cannot give up. You can't give up." So I began pushing on a hatch cover and it was closed. It was locked. The water pressure...I couldn't open it! I swam to the other hatch cover. That was closed. That wouldn't budge. It was real dark, pitch-black. What I didn't know was that the barge was going over me. There was noise like you wouldn't

believe! I was rolling around; everything was rolling because the whole boat was underneath the barge. I was deep under water, holding my breath. They say that you can't hold your breath longer than three minutes. But I held it.

It was pitch-black, you know; there was *no place* to go. I kept looking for light. And then all of a sudden I saw a bright, bright light and it was like somebody *pushed* me! It felt like somebody was pushing me right up through the water. I shot up so fast. I just bounced out of the water, and then I saw the barge going by. I was on the side of the barge. I saw men standing on the barge; their eyes were big as saucers. The boat had cracked up with me inside it. It was all in pieces. I saw pieces of the boat all around me. The guys on the barge were waving to me. I said, "Help!" They screamed, "Yeah, we see you!"

And there was my boyfriend; he was way at the other end of the barge. They were pulling him up. He had lost his swimming trunks. He was naked. But I was way in front of the barge now, so they threw me a life preserver. I don't know how to swim, I can only do a dog paddle for a real long time, which, when you think about it is the most amazing thing of all, that this happened to someone who can't even swim. I held on to the life preserver, and they yanked it. I could have been sucked under the water, under the boat, by the force of the pull from the boat going by me, but I literally walked myself up the side of the barge. My bikini top was around my neck and the bottom was around one ankle. I didn't realize until much later that my feet were all cut up by barnacle scrapes. But that's the only thing that happened to me!

They were just staring at us like creatures from the deep. I was walking around in circles for minutes, thinking, "God! What just happened to me?"

I often think about the force that made me pop up, the light I saw, and the feeling that somebody pushed me to the surface. It makes me think I'm here to accomplish something, that I have a destiny to fulfill.

—MARIA ZABOREK, HOUSTON, TEXAS, HUMAN RESOURCES ASSISTANT FOR AMOCO

It is in the very act of opening ourselves to the divine presence, whether now or at the final moment of our life, that God can reach in, kiss us on the head, and make us conscious of His unlimited Goodness. That's His way.

In fear we never rest, but in faith we rest in angels' arms.

THE CUSHION

About four years ago, while I was still married to my abusive husband, I had an experience the details of which shall never leave me.

We had been arguing because the sudden mood struck me to go dancing with him on a Wednesday night. We lived on an Air Force base and frequented the club there from time to time. But he, being a rather "routine type" of person, saw my spontaneous idea to be nothing short of frivolous.

An argument ensued, turning into hitting and hurling. He opened the garage door. He lifted me up above his head—I am five foot one and he is six feet tall—and literally threw me out of the house, down a couple of steps to the garage floor.

This is what happened, though. As I was descending to the hard, cold cement, I felt a big round cushion of air slipped under me, and when I actually hit the ground, it was painless! I believe that if that had not transpired I would have been aching with back injuries and pain thereafter.

There are countless other incidents that may seem insignificant to others, but in retrospect these experiences have me believing that angels truly live.

—AMELIA A. WISE, HONOLULU, HAWAII

Angels deliver messages of certainty and hope, encouraging us to let go of limitations and to embrace the unlimited values of

Heaven. They are incorporeal agents of hope in an all too physical and dangerous world.

The angels are here to give us a reason to live when we want to die, to remind us that we have friends when we feel we have none, that there is a place where courage is always in full blossom, no matter how we tremble and cannot move, that there are beings around us ready to explain every mystery of life, if we will only listen… and that we really can fly if we want to.

Your soul has to be involved in trusting and faith in order to prove the miraculous, to call forth the invisible heroic forces of good fortune and well-being and to invoke the angels.

There are literally angelic beings with no other purpose than to assist and love you. They have no needs and have no other function. They have no personal desire, only unlimited love, power, goodness, and wisdom, which they offer to you. All we need to do is ask.

God is ever watching. The Angels are ever present. Finding God is easy. It is inevitable. Whenever we ask for Him, He is already there.

THE TRUCK IN THE ALLEY

One day when I was living in Manhattan, I was daydreaming, kinda walking around in Greenwich Village. I found myself wandering into this alley where they have those loading dock spaces between the high-rises where the trucks unload. I really didn't know what I was doing because I had been very deep in thought. I had some problems; I was thinking. Anyhow, while I was in there, suddenly I saw this truck backing toward me. It was so big that it pretty much took up the whole space. I couldn't get out on the left or right. I couldn't jump up, because it was pretty high. I could have lain down on the floor, but that's one thing I didn't think of. It's kind of an extreme idea, to lie down when there's a truck backing toward you.

And so I was paralyzed with fear. I couldn't do anything. I couldn't even scream. The only thing, since I have a very strong belief in God, the only thing I said was "Oh, Lord, you've got to send me one of your angels to help me now!" That's all I remember saying, and the next thing, this truck backs all the way up at me and really kind of brushes me. It didn't hit me but kinda brushed me, and then it stopped. The truck moved forward, and the driver jumped out, and he was white like a sheet! He said, "Oh my God! I heard a voice in my truck vibrating, 'STOP!' I usually back up, but it told me to stop. I would have squashed you!"

"I heard it! 'STOP! NOW!' It was so loud! I was in such shock, I stopped instantly." The first thing he did was, he jumped out of his truck. And then he saw me, and it flipped him out!

95

He knew that something supernatural had happened. I said, "All I did is I asked God to send me an angel." And he said, "Oh, this angel sure has a loud voice!"

When it was all over, he invited me for a cup of coffee, and he said, "You know, you just made a believer out of me! If things like this can happen... I heard the voice in my truck so loud, it just stopped me in my tracks! The whole truck was vibrating!" And I said, "I guess maybe angels have such loud voices because they need to reach you! I feel so blessed that someone actually heard my prayer!"

What I felt was a sense of incredible joy, because I knew that someone was watching over me. I had a sense that the promise "I am always with you, and you will never be alone" is true. It's a wonderful feeling of being watched over. I never questioned if I was saved only because I cried out. Or was it because I hadn't fulfilled my destiny yet? I think a prayer always helps. There are millions of stories when people cry out at the last second before something happens to them, and then a miracle takes place instead.

—BRIDGET NEWTON, LAS VEGAS, NEVADA,
RESERVATIONS CLERK AT BALLY'S HOTEL

Faith is part of the great force that keeps the planets in their orbits and our hearts pumping, the clouds moving, and the sun shining. It is perfectly natural. Faith is a part of God's nature. We must protect, nurture, and reveal our natural faith by continually making use of it. An angel's faith is eternally pure and fresh, because an angel endlessly employs it. Flying is an act of faith.

So many angel stories prove that sometimes a simple call is all that's needed to bring angels. Call on your angels in bad times and in good. Don't wait for disaster to prove their existence. Attract them now.

Above all, always remember you are not alone. You do have a guardian angel—in fact, many angels—always near. Expect an angel as you help yourself and offer assistance to those around you.

We allow or disallow our experience of angels.

Two Tons of Steel

This happened at the Budd Manufacturing Company in north-east Philadelphia when I worked there. One day I was standing near a crane that was moving a load—two tons of steel sheets. I saw the crane hit the side of another big machine on the ground, which caused the load to tilt. I jumped, but I felt I was actually lifted up above the ground about five feet and somehow, I don't know how, I landed on top of the whole two tons of steel. I could hardly believe it happened. It was a miracle. I immediately thanked God and my guardian angel for the miracle I received!

—Joseph Di Emidio, Philadelphia, Pennsylvania, retired

The angels are here for us to acknowledge or not, as we choose. As with everything else in life, we are free to perceive and accept great meaning or none at all.

We can call it luck, beating the odds, our turn for good fortune, or we can bend our heads and give thanks to That which controls and guides all things.

To appreciate angels, it is important to appreciate life.

Becoming aware of angels will make us happier people and help us relax. We are constantly being invited, being groomed, cared for, answered, and ushered toward our destinies, for better or worse.

Angels are a part of the cosmic glue that fills the gaps in our thinking. There are times when there is just no logical reason for our plight, nor explanation for our safety, either. No matter what, when we understand angels, all is well.

THE NEW YORK CITY BUS

I've had a lot of experiences before where something made me turn or stop at the last minute, but they are very vague and most of them I forget. The one that I really remember happened about four and a half years ago on a New York City bus going down Second Avenue. I was sitting in a seat by myself toward the front when something told me to move. It was a pretty empty bus, so for no real reason I just moved back a few seats and across to a double-seater. There was an elderly lady sitting a couple of seats in front, near where I was originally sitting.

After I sat down, a few seconds later a big cement truck came barreling into the bus, and the window over the seat that she was sitting in was broken in half and she got cut. She was upset, but she didn't get hurt severely. But the seat I had been sitting in was basically covered with glass—that was where most of the impact was. I said, "Wow!" That's about all I could say. I was in shock,

and I was grateful for not getting badly hurt by the crash. It was interesting.... Something told me to move. That's all I know.

I think I said, "Oh, thank you, God, thank you for helping me out." But I don't really remember, to be honest with you. I imagine I acknowledged the presence of the Divine intervening in my life at the time. In any case, it stayed with me, and I acknowledge it now.

—DEBRA PARKER, HOLLYWOOD, CALIFORNIA,
TV WRITER, DIRECTOR, AND PRODUCER

It's important to listen through our intuition... to what heavenly forces are saying to us. When we get a message, it is absolutely urgent that we pay attention to it and do what we're supposed to do. Or else, we can step in the wrong place and have a real problem.

When bad things happen, we can use them as reminders to stay more in touch, listen to our intuition, trust it, listen to messages when they are sent, and follow all instructions as they are given.

The angels may tell you to meditate, take a class, speak to someone, read a certain book, go to a lecture, pray a certain prayer, make a call, turn on the radio or the TV at a certain moment, leave the house, turn a corner, take a particular vacation, or go home a certain way.

Why don't angels always show themselves? They are neither shy, nor secretive, nor fearful of public attention. They stay hidden for our benefit, so that we don't come to depend on them too much or give up our own power and freedom of choice.

Can miracles save us? If we fly, will God catch us? If we rise into a new way of being, will Heaven take us in?

There are times when it would take an angel to resolve a problem. There are times when only a miracle will do.

Angels have no fear of earthly problems. They have abilities far greater than our own and are not limited by this world at all.

Angels live in the realm of all perfection.

THE HELICOPTER

This happened on Sunday, August 19, 1990, when I was flying. I'm a bush pilot, and I do special high-altitude work with helicopters, a lot of remote work up in Alaska, around the Rocky Mountains, and all over Colorado, Wyoming, Montana, Idaho, Utah, Arizona, and Costa Rica. One Sunday afternoon, a beautiful, clear sunny day in Wyoming, we were working in the wilderness area around Yellowstone National Park.

I'd worked a month straight; it was my last day of the contract, and it was my last flight, doing survey work, flying a

helicopter, taking a survey crew around. It's an all-day job, six or seven days a week, that lasts for months. I landed at about 8,700 feet to pick up a crew and fly them into town. The support crew had already gone back to the town of Meteefle, where we were all staying.

I landed on top of the mountain and radioed the crew: "You need to hurry because there is a rain shower coming down the valley." Because it's so dry out there, anytime you get rain you get lightning and I didn't want to have to fly through any lightning and rain. The guys hurried, they got in, we took off. I accelerated down the side of the mountain because I wanted to lose a couple thousand feet of altitude and then leveled off around 7,000 feet. I set up a slow descent to make it to Meteefle.

About two minutes after takeoff, the helicopter started to shake a bit. I recognized the vibration as a problem with air in one of the hydraulic adapters in the rotor system, so I took the control stick and I wiggled it, which usually gets the vibration to quit. About fifteen seconds later, it started again. So I wiggled the stick again, but this time it didn't go away. I turned off the hydraulic to the unit; it actually made it worse. So I turned the hydraulics back on.

Then all of a sudden it started getting worse and worse. The helicopter started shaking violently.... I was trying to hang on to it, but the control stick started following the vibration; it was whipping around in a big triangular pattern. I got huge black-and-blue marks between my legs, it was so violent. I was getting scared, terribly scared. The whole sheath started shaking horribly, and my crew of six started screaming and moaning. The vibrations got so bad that the emergency locator transmitter

went off. Everyone was screaming, and the helicopter was making an incredible racket. I had a whistling noise in my ears, and then the thought came through my mind, "I just want to hit something, the side of a mountain, and get it over," because if we lost a rotor blade or transmission we were gonna fall four thousand feet and crash into the rocks. I couldn't do an emergency landing because we were over this real windy creek with huge boulders the size of Volkswagens. You know, there was just no place to set down, and I figured I had only about 5 percent control left. The control stick was just going nuts.

Then what happened is that I started getting a real real bad case of tunnel vision... which is what human physiology does, I've since learned, when you can't handle too much stress. I started losing reference. I couldn't see the window frame. I couldn't see an inch of my panel. All I could see was light ahead of me...a point of light outside in front of me. I knew there was a field outside the valley, but I didn't even know where.

So I just said an instant prayer. It was the most powerful affirmation I ever said in my life because I had so much determination behind it. I said, *"Everything is gonna be okay!"* I tried to get myself centered in my mind. And then it seemed like time stopped. The next thing I knew, I heard the resonance of the helicopter change. If you fly a lot, you'll notice that when you get real close to the ground in a helicopter, it gets quieter, and the resonance, the vibration, changes frequently. So I automatically started pulling back on the stick.

The people were all still screaming. I asked one of 'em later what I was doing. And the guy says, "You were busy!" But I don't remember that. All's I know is somehow the helicopter flew

104

from the point I lost visual reference, to this beautiful, fantastically flat field about five miles away. I couldn't see outside at all, so how could I fly the helicopter? Not only that but, amazingly, we turned about thirty degrees and lined up with the most perfect flat spot in Wyoming. It was so hard just to keep the helicopter from rolling over. There's no way I could have flown five miles and kept the helicopter right side up.

Now I've never told anyone this story the way I'm telling it because they would've all thought I was nuts. The stick was still going around in this big triangular pattern, beating my leg and trying to break my arm, and then I remember feeling an impact. Then I lost consciousness.

Apparently I hit the instrument panel with my chin, and it knocked me out. Then we flipped upside down and flew about sixty feet. We landed upside down, going backward, and caught on fire. Everybody got out except me. When I came to, something seemed strange. I was upside down, hanging in my seat. I couldn't get my seat belt loose. Finally two guys realized I was still in the machine and they came back. One guy had real long, blond hair. He didn't want to burn his hair, but he came in anyway and he got me out.

The machine was totally destroyed. I have pictures of it looking like a charred pile of rubble. I didn't know what I had experienced; I had never run across it. I know we were still over the valley when I lost consciousness, when I lost sight—when I lost vision. From the time I lost consciousness until we hit the ground, I didn't fly the helicopter! I couldn't have. I had no visual reference.

In the end, I had six passengers, and everybody walked away

from the accident. They were just totally amazed, and so were the people that came up after the accident. I had a big gash underneath my chin, but I was the only one who got a cut out of the whole thing.

I just know that... that my guide—my angel... whatever you want to call it—flew the aircraft for me. I didn't use that on my NTSB report, because they would have thought I was crazy. Actually, I told my wife, and she said, "If I were you, I wouldn't repeat that to anyone."

I just knew that when I got centered and I said that everything was gonna be okay, all I had to do was surrender. It was like, "Okay, God, it's all Yours. Take over." But like I said, other than my wife, I've never told this story to anyone.

—ERIC BOYCE, ST. PETER, MISSOURI, HELICOPTER BUSH PILOT

Angels are a good explanation for the miraculous experiences that bring out that special voice within us that only ever manages to utter two words—"Thank God."

Angels come only when invited, whether consciously or not. They have nothing but true friendship to offer, and they ask nothing but trust.

We are not in a master/slave bond with the Divine but in an integral union. We are as much a part of It as It is of us. We are all made of the same stuff, each of us a slice of the infinite pie.

The most advantageous use of free will is reuniting in all respects with our own perfect essence. We can make use of our own inner power in the right way and achieve marvelous results. For every step in this direction we are given our wings.

❖   ❖   ❖

Angels can educate us in the reality of miracles. It is a part of their greater assignment. It makes them happy when we accept.

It is through our many joy-filled windows of receptivity that angels dare to fly right into our hearts.

When angels appear in our lives in whatever form we accept them, we see that virtually all known rules can be broken or, rather, instantly dissolved by divine ones.

Just Passing Through

My angel experience occurred when I was twenty years old, around 1973. One morning on my way to work I was driving on Interstate 85 in Greenville, South Carolina, when it began to rain slightly, just enough to cause the road to become slippery. I drove a '72 Mustang Mach I, and after I braked lightly for a vehicle ahead of me, the car began swerving violently, spinning me around in the road. When I finally stopped, I found myself across both lanes of the southbound traffic. I looked to my left, and coming toward me at seventy-plus miles an hour was a semi truck, frantically blowing his horn.

I remember looking over my shoulder at a man in a pickup who had pulled over when I started spinning. He had an expression of terror, even grief, and buried his face in his hands to avoid seeing me struck by the approaching semi.

But suddenly my own fear was overwhelmed by the strongest sense of total calm and relief I have ever experienced. It was such peace I almost felt I wasn't even part of this earth. And in the seat next to me was the Source.... I can't say I visually saw an angel, but it was there. And, as difficult to believe as this may be, when I looked to my right, that semi was on the other side of me, still traveling down the road in that same left lane. He had no way around me, except through divine intervention.

I am a college-educated wife and mother of two children, very active in church, school, and community activities. As a younger person I felt "different" when expressing "angel experiences," and I still feel timid about voicing what I know as true and actual happenings. I have often been painfully shy. I used to share my angel experiences with family members. They always indulged me, but I also knew they felt I was "different," too. Sadly, I keep such experiences tucked away. Thanks for listening.

—Name Withheld

Angels tend to boggle the mind. Part of their purpose is to get us away from our linear thinking, from our materialism and intellectualism and back into the greater spaces of our virtually limitless potential.

As human beings we have the privilege of looking at the mirror of life from both sides. Our angel encounters prove it is our choice to see the deeper reality of our oneness with God or the false impression of duality. Our angel encounters prove to us that the separations we fear are illusory.

Angels prove their presence in subtle and ordinary, dramatic, miraculous, and sometimes unthinkable, ways.

Throughout the ages angels have appeared as messengers, rescuers, guides, and friends in times of danger, but they are with us all the time.

THE SNOWSTORM

I was moving some stuff for a guy I knew who owned a clothing store on my block on East Sixtieth Street, in New York, to a house way out on the tip of Long Island. It was the middle of winter, and we had just had a very big snowstorm. There was snow everywhere, and it was very cold, but we loaded up my old Ford van and took it out there.

By the time I was ready to go back, it seemed like the battery was dead. But what was actually wrong was that the alternator was dead, which I didn't know at the time means the whole car is running straight off the battery without recharging, so it won't run for long. The battery has only a very short life left in it, and it's got to run the whole car. Basically, you can't drive a car without an alternator.

So I started back—a three-hour trip to Manhattan. Knowing I had some sort of mechanical problem, I tried to take side streets, the old roads instead of the expressway. Actually, I got lost and I found myself going all through different towns. Finally I got back on the Long Island Expressway, where I kept seeing cars embanked in the snow on the side of the roads. I knew I needed a miracle. I decided to pray for one. To make a long story short, by the time I got back to Manhattan, it had actually taken me an hour and a half less than it took going out!

It makes no sense at all. I made it back without running out of juice in the battery. I found out the next day that there was no alternator at all, so I shouldn't have even been able to drive.

But it happened in an emergency, so that makes it an angel

story. I asked for a miracle and I got one. You can get what you ask for.

—THOMAS CAMPBELL, NEW YORK AND LOS ANGELES,
ACTOR AND BUSINESSMAN

We can accept the personal, unconditional support of our angels and achieve great things.

When we are moved to confront treacherous opponents, we can hang on to our divine inner strength, never forgetting for a moment the guardians of power and grace that surround us. When we surrender, our power does not come from our human selves alone; it is the power of the holy angels flowing through us into our lives.

Heavenly instructions need no translation. They speak directly to the soul. When we have an angel experience, we understand perfectly. Angels never explain themselves. All angelic lessons are understood exactly as they are given.

113

THE KILLER BEES

My apartment was invaded last year by hundreds of killer bees. I awoke early, walked into the kitchen, and there they were all around me. My angels kept me cool, calm, and collected. I quietly backed out of the kitchen, sealed off the rest of the house, got my mom out of bed, dressed, and left through the living room. The kitchen and living room were one room. The bees remained buzzing all around the kitchen and living room but made no attempt to attack us as we exited the front door in trepidation and relief.

The city sent workers in with masks and bee-repellent clothing, and they sprayed my house, killing all the bees, which apparently had nested in my air-conditioning unit.

But I will never forget having walked into their midst and not being stung! I am allergic to bee stings and insect bites of any kind. I am also deathly afraid of bees. On that morning, however, a tremendous calm enveloped me, and I escaped without one single bee attacking—lots of angels protecting me. I kept a bag of dead bees as visible confirmation of a really incredible event and as evidence for my boss, who claimed she had heard every dumb excuse there was for being late to work.

I believe in angels. They have been with me since childhood. Sometimes I lose touch with them, but at other times, I am intensely conscious of their presence. Even when I am not communing with them, I always know they are protecting me and mine.

Angels have brought me through earthquakes, hurricanes,

serious illness, freak car accidents, and near accidents. The best jobs I have ever had I obtained through angels. I have been flat broke and didn't know how I would eat and, by the power of God's angels, pulled a five-dollar bill out of my coat pocket, which had been empty a few minutes before. There have been many miraculous interventions in my life by God's great angels. Angels? *Yes!*

—JOAN MANN, VAN NUYS, CALIFORNIA

Angels don't do parlor tricks. They are not showmen or a part of some cosmic circus act. They are governed by the very Highest, so they have no need to impress, they have no desire for credibility and don't need our faith or even our trust.

Our little troubles attract the attention of our angels. Whether self-inflicted or from the outside, the angels tend to our pain. They surround us, unseen, awaiting an opportunity to make their presence known.

THE REFRIGERATOR

My first angel experience happened when I was six years old.
My girlfriend and I went down into the basement of our house,
the laundry room, and it had some old appliances that weren't
being used. We were pretending like we were hiding. We
looked in the dryer. No, the dryer's too small. The washer—I
looked at that thing in the middle. Nope. Can't get in there.
The oven—well, too small. But the old refrigerator—perfect
place!

So we get in and I get on the bottom shelf, and we're both
just kind of sitting there, I don't know why. We were not
really talking anymore, and my foot was tapping on the door.
Then, suddenly, I remember seeing the light get smaller and
smaller and smaller and then just—*click*. The door clicked
shut. It was a refrigerator made in the fifties, the kind that
they discontinued because children were being suffocated in
them. It had a steel latch, where the handle went over the
steel pin that stuck out, and the door could be opened only
from the outside.

We just started pushing, and then the shelf broke and she
was on top of me and our legs were getting cut up and everything. We were pushing frantically with our hands on the
rubber, but this wasn't a refrigerator that could be pushed open.
It was just a big, bulky, heavy thing.

And then, for no reason at all, the door flew open! When I
told my mother what had happened, a look came over her face,

116

and without hesitation she told me my guardian angel must have opened the door for us. I believed her. I still do.

—Monica Marie Downer, Los Angeles, California,
TELEVISION PRODUCER

The mystical is right here. Angels are a brilliant part of the fabric of spirituality that is everywhere. They play a role in everyone's life. They are a part of us in the same magical way that we are a part of everything.

Simple moments are holy for one in search of the Divine. What is sacred and precious may go unnoticed because it is so entirely natural.

In little ways, we're all like angels sometimes.

THE POST OFFICE ANGEL

I was in a bind to get a portion of my master's thesis proposal to another town via overnight mail. I was certain that some "express mail" existed. I went to the post office with high hopes but was told, "No, we can't do that." I pleaded that I only needed to get these papers to a certain town by ten o'clock the next morning. No go! I returned from the post office window in mild, quiet dejection, but as I turned to go out the door, a middle-aged woman approached me and said, "We're going through that town today. Can we take that for you?" I said to her, "Oh! I believe in angels, and I believe I've just met one!" She took my proposal 240 miles, drove it to the Nursing Department of the university, and personally handed it to my thesis chair! I sent her an angel pin and I pray for her—how's that for a story?

—MARTY, A BOISE, IDAHO, *REGISTERED NURSE AND NURSE EDUCATOR*

We ought to have a "good news" channel where daily stories of outstanding human virtue are featured, true stories—the ones that happen in our world every day—of heroic acts of faith, kindness, and selfless service to each other… with hourly angel reports.

There are often times that with a little Divine guidance we become the earthly "angels" acting in accord with intuitive messages from beyond ourselves, from that part of us which is a part of Heaven.

When we act as angels, we are left in the hero's position, scratching our heads and wondering how it was possible that we saved the day. By remaining anonymous, the angels show us that it doesn't really matter who takes credit, because we are all a part of God.

THE WAYWARD VAN

I was living in California about 1967, and I was dating a girl in New York. I flew in to see her, and one day we're walking down the street in Alphabet City, on the Lower East Side, on Avenue C and about Eighth Street. Bad neighborhood, especially in 1967. Walking south on Avenue C, which is a one-way street going north, we were just walking along normally. You know, you walk in New York and you don't pay attention. We're walking side by side when all of a sudden I spotted a truck coming toward us, at least seven blocks away, which is really impossible to see in New York.

A few minutes later, I glanced at her, I glanced at the approaching truck again, and without thinking I just pushed her as hard as I could, away from me. As I pushed her, the truck collided with a van that was parked right next to us. She went flying away from me, parallel to the building, which was some eight feet away. But as I pushed her, she reached out for my hand, wondering why I pushed her. I heard her say, "Why?" with both hands stretched out. The truck passed between us exactly the width of how far we were apart. It broke a little bottle I had in my pocket, that's how close it came to me. The force lifted her up and chopped off three fingers, just the tips of her fingers. It grabbed her fingertips, and she went flying in the air as the truck went right into the brick wall.

120

And I picked up her fingers, wrapped them up, and we rushed to the hospital. They sewed them back on, and she was fine. If I hadn't pushed her, either she would have been dead, or we both would have been dead, or maybe I would have been dead.

I saw it all happening. I knew exactly what was going to happen. I don't know how, but I did. What makes it an angel story is that something made me notice this van coming at us, because I was caught up in talking to her, not really looking around at the streets at all. I felt like something was nudging at me. Something kept on bothering me to pay attention. And then something told me to shove her with all my might for no real reason at all. And then I found out the reason. That's what I really think. Angels don't rescue you, per se. They allow you to see what's going on, like giving someone a little nudge.

—STANLEY NEWTON, VENICE, CALIFORNIA, WORLD-CLASS
PROFESSIONAL PHOTOGRAPHER

We all have "inside friends"… our own "A list."

When we are called to act as angels, it is because we have earned the right, the privilege. We have aligned ourselves with the holy forces by following the Higher Will without suspicion, without doubt, without argument or resistance.

Angel stories, like miracles, are not to be figured out or analyzed, except by faith. And faith is an acceptance of things unseen, based on information collected solely by the heart.

THE TOBOGGAN

I have the capacity to forget real unpleasant things, but I remember, as a child, I went to this horrible, horrible boarding school in Canada where they beat you every week. You had to line up. They had leather straps. It was a big, old, cold, and dark stone building with lots of hallways. This place was horrible. I cried almost every night, I felt so alone.

Anyway, at this boarding school, it was a very cold wintry day. There was a lot of ice on a huge hill that went down to the river. There had been a lot of snow, so the river was raging. It was a very gray day, and it was getting dark and time to go in.

The bottom of the hill was a good distance from the river; that's why we were allowed to go down it. There were some other kids there, too. I was tobogganing down this small mountain when my toboggan started absolutely flying because of the ice, and suddenly, I knew I was going into the river. I was going at such a speed that I couldn't stop or divert myself. I knew that if I plunged in I would be drowned. I felt so much fear I was frozen stiff. I was just speeding directly toward the river and I knew I couldn't stop the momentum of the sled.

Right at the height of my panic, I don't know exactly what happened, I didn't hit a bump or anything, but I suddenly went

to the left. The toboggan just turned and stopped all by itself. I don't know how to this day. I couldn't understand how or why it turned or how it stopped, either. But I didn't go in the river. If I had, there would have been no way I could ever have come out. I would have been drowned.

I remember thinking right away, "How did that happen?" As a child I always knew how strange it was, but I had no way to think about it. But as I grew up I began to think the explanation is that I had "help." I can see that now. In retrospect, I see even in that terrible place I had a guardian angel on the job. I believe it was a divine force. Like a miracle. I know I was saved from death that day. I guess I wasn't so alone, after all.

I think we can all go back to our childhood and recall times like that.

—ANNIE HELM, PASADENA, CALIFORNIA, ACTRESS, ARTIST, WRITER

We won't need to ask for them. Our angels will just be there.

Trying to explain a miracle is like trying to explain death or birth. Your mind just doesn't know what to do about it. It's not intellectual. It's something that affects your soul.

The human mind may run in different directions trying to interpret angelic events in another way, but it will soon tire and give out… making way for the Divine.

BABY OUT THE WINDOW

This was September 1993, and my third son, Michael, who was then eighteen months old, was up in our third-floor playroom, which is a converted attic, with a bunch of other children. We happened to be having a dinner party that night, and we had a baby-sitter up there with the children. All the adults were down in the dining room. It was about eight-thirty and pitch-black outside.

We have an old brick Georgian house, it's a very tall three-story house. As we were having dessert, the baby-sitter came screaming down the stairs, "Michael!" and she ran out the front door. I knew he hadn't gone outside in the dark—he wouldn't do that—and so I immediately knew he had fallen from a third-floor window. She was screaming and screaming, "Michael!" and I ran right behind her screaming, "Call 911!"

There were no lights on this side of the house, it was pitch-black, but I could hear him crying and, somehow, I found him in the dark. I put my hands under his body in the dark, and I could feel that his head was lying against bricks—my neighbors have a little flower garden there lined in bricks. He was lying against it, kind of on the side, but his head was right against the bricks. He was conscious and he was crying. It was still pitch-black, so we couldn't see anything. People were saying, "Don't move him, don't move him," but I couldn't help but put my arms under him and pick him up a little bit. I just couldn't help myself. It seemed like an eternity before the paramedics got there.

The paramedics couldn't believe he was conscious, couldn't

124

believe he was crying, couldn't believe the child wasn't bleeding and didn't have a mark anywhere on his body. Not a bump, not a bruise; he never showed any signs of soreness. But we didn't realize how miraculous it was until we got to the hospital and all the medical people started telling us, "You know that you have a guardian angel at your house. It's a miracle that this child wasn't hurt."

The paramedics could not believe the condition he was in. He fought them, you know. They put him on one of those boards and he was fighting so hard in the ambulance going to the hospital, they taped his body down with thick duct tape. They taped his head and arms and legs down with it to keep him from moving because they felt he should have had...if not broken bones, then internal injuries. The paramedics said he should have been unconscious.

The emergency room personnel started checking him out, and then they said, "You better call your pediatrician. There might be something wrong here, you know, a neck injury or something." So we called our pediatrician, who examined his body three times, and I'm talking looked in his nose, his mouth, examined his tongue, his teeth, looked in his ears, examined his toes, every part of his body three times, and then they gave him a tranquilizer, a sedative, and put him into the CAT machine. I mean they put a thing on him to see if there was blood in his urine.

They were doing all these horrible tests to him. Actually, we think the tests hurt him more than the fall did. But they thought surely there was some injury to the child. We stayed overnight in the hospital, and every hour they checked his vital

signs. They woke us up. He was perfectly normal. We were released the next day, but I had nurses and doctors visiting me while we were there that night and in the morning. They all wanted to see this miracle child. The people in the hospital kept saying, "You have a guardian angel at your house. Your child was saved in some way."

I never have had any real brush with death like this before, but I've always sort of felt somebody was looking out for me. And we just felt that yes, perhaps Michael was saved by a guardian angel. As my housekeeper said, he was carried down in the angel's arms, because his body was uninjured and the breath was not even knocked out of him. The baby-sitter was a teenager, had been with us for a few years, and she just about had a nervous breakdown over it. She couldn't drive home; my husband drove her. And her parents came right over to the hospital that night. It wasn't her fault at all. On the third floor, the windows go to the floor level. He must have stepped into the window, pushed on it, leaned against the screen, and just went out.

We're not real religious people, but we felt that Michael was saved by the grace of God. We really do. He was just...you know...totally unhurt. We have three pretty wild and crazy boys. But we really haven't had any bad things happen. But this one was, we feel, a brush with death, and we were saved. I mean it really makes you wonder how people can not think that there's a higher power up there.

—A DEERFIELD, ILLINOIS, FULL-TIME MOM, NAME WITHHELD

126

An angel encounter is life-changing, giving rise to greater faith and advancing peace of mind forever.

Angels are the many winged hands of God

There are so many exceptions to insecurity and pain that even to the blindest among us there is a deeper rule. Angels follow this deeper rule of unconditional love.

We are all standing together in the newness of creation dreaming we are not a part of nature, but we are. We are as much a part of living as the wind and the sea and the light of the stars coming from millions of miles away. Realization is our ticket to the infinite.

CLEARING THE AISLE

I used to have a store in New York on First Avenue across from Maxwell's Plum. We did latex transfers on T-shirts. One afternoon, the store was packed with people, thank God. It wasn't that big of a store, I mean not huge like some storefronts in New York, but it had a huge plate-glass window in the front.

All of a sudden I got a feeling that there were too many people around. So I kinda cleared a spot. Just as I got done clearing an aisle, all of a sudden I moved, I leaned over for a second into the aisle and I heard an explosion. Everyone in the store turned around. I said, "What was that?" They all basically said, "I don't know." I looked behind me, and there was a big piece of metal stuck in the wall. It was from the transmission, the gear cluster of a truck. It had exploded off a truck that was driving down the street, went right through the plate-glass window…breezed by me. I heard and felt it go "*pffft.*" I don't know why I didn't think it was anything. And it stuck in the wall, within inches of me—a piece of metal right behind my head. It didn't even crack the window; it just made a hole.

When I leaned over, it was like something put pressure on me, moved me off to the side, I mean, I never did that before, clearing the aisle. I like the store crowded, you know, who wants to clear most of the store?

—*STANLEY NEWTON, VENICE, CALIFORNIA,*
PROFESSIONAL PHOTOGRAPHER

What are angels and how can we find them? Not with slide rules and investigative reports, but with love, an observant eye, and a little appreciation.

We are not alone. That is the primary message.

Whenever we listen to an angel story, the questions always emerge: Would I do that? and, Could that ever happen to me? Yes, it could, and in your better moments, of course, you would. Because within you is that very same Holy Spirit which powers and guides the greatest of angels.

OUT OF BODY

This is a weird story, I know it is. But I'm going to tell you just what happened the way it happened. Let me preface this story by telling you that I had experiences when I was younger where I came out of my body and floated above it. Usually the thing that I remember most is coming out of my body and being scared, then pulling myself back in. This particular evening I was napping, and somehow, I didn't remember leaving my body at all, but I found myself suddenly out. And I remember I said, "Ooh, I'm out of my body!" And I pulled myself back in. I wasn't aware of how long I had been out.

This was when I was in college. I had a relationship with a

129

guy who was supposed to pick me up for school the next
morning. He never showed up. I had to get to class, so I went in
myself. Later I found out he wasn't in school. It turns out that he
was in a really bad accident the evening before. I learned the
next day that it had occurred at pretty much exactly the same
time that I was pulling myself back into my body.

He was on a deserted road on the north shore of Long
Island. He had one of those really big pickup trucks with the big
wheels that were in vogue then. And he flipped the truck,
tumbling over front to back, and he was thrown out of his truck.
What he told me later was that he came out of his body and he
looked at himself lying in the road in a pool of blood, and he
remembered thinking, "Oh, boy! Now what?" What had
happened was his skull had split open. He actually lost his ear.
He said he looked at himself and then something made him turn
around and he saw *me* in the road...down the road. I said,
"Follow me."

So he pulled himself back into his body and he followed me
home. I mean, he physically kept following me down through
the streets until he made it home. He said he just got back into
his body and he made his body walk, and he actually walked
home physically, a couple of miles. This is a man who they
couldn't believe lived, who they couldn't believe wasn't brain-
dead, who made it through.

He says I'm an angel. Anyway, that's what he says. I don't
have any recollection of it and I don't claim to be an angel. All I
know is, it was really weird to me, because that night I did have
the experience of coming back into my body but no recollection
of being out of it. So it was kind of strange, and we weren't

together long after that. Maybe we were just together to have this experience.

—DEBRA PARKER, LOS ANGELES, CALIFORNIA, TV WRITER,
DIRECTOR, AND PRODUCER

There's an "angelsoul" inside each one of us. Recognizing that part of us and giving it the greatest value and credit and appreciation we can give is what will alter our lives and bring back the pure meaning and wonder of living.

And as we creep back to the source of Goodness, tired, bedraggled, clasping our hearts to hold the pieces lest they fly away and leave us, they are present—halos aglow, laughing, light streaming forth, pronouncing our freedom, certain we are saved.

Angels are present all the time. They don't sleep or eat. They don't take vacations and they have no stresses from which to escape.

THE SCREAM

W hen I was in college, my boyfriend and I were taking a long drive. It was late at night, and we both fell asleep. We were veering into oncoming traffic. Suddenly I awoke, and for no apparent reason I screamed as loudly as I could, "WAKE UP!" I don't know what made me do it.

It was so bizarre. My eyes weren't even open. I think a passing angel made me scream from a sound sleep and then woke me up. My boyfriend got control of the car, swerved to avoid a car in the opposite lane, and thanked me profusely. Neither one of us could explain our luck except to say we had help from somewhere else. That would have been the end of us. I thank my guardian angel for helping us that night.

—LOS ANGELES, CALIFORNIA, SECRETARY AND MOTHER,
NAME WITHHELD

God is doing business with the stars and planets all the time, handling the intricacies of cosmic circulation, government, science, and every other field, never losing focus for a moment.

Our business affairs pale in the light of His. He is doing every job. Nothing is too great or small for His attention. We would do well to simply be on His staff, ever mindful of His presence, attuning our actions and our hearts to His will.

To accept our angels is to break the straps that challenge human life and to rise into the miraculous.

TODD'S RIDE HOME

The night of the '94 L. A. earthquake, I was sleeping at my then-girlfriend's house, and the clock struck three. For no particular reason, I said, "Eva…I'm going home." And she said, "Okay." And I got up and went home. As I pulled into the house, I normally open the gate, drive into the driveway, pull into the garage, close the garage door, and walk into the house. But for an unknown reason this time for the very first time in eight months, I parked at the gate. I just didn't feel like going in. So then I went to bed, and the earthquake struck at four-thirty or so, a little over an hour later.

My house had lots of damage. The chimney collapsed and fell across the driveway. Had I been parked in the driveway, the chimney would have fallen on top of the car. Had I been parked in the garage, I wouldn't have been able to get out, because the bricks from the chimney were strewn across the driveway. Plus, we didn't have any power. It's a power garage. I wouldn't have been able to open the garage door, and the car would have been stuck in there. But since the car was out front, all I did after the earthquake was go outside, put my dog into the car, back up, and go. Also, my dog was sleeping with me on the bed. Had I not been home, she would have been sleeping in her bed, which was crushed by fallen furniture.

It was like a whisper in the ear, a feeling, a voice in my head, an intuition. It was just a feeling. I have no idea where the thought came from to break my routine, but I'm glad, very glad, I was listening.

—TODD FELDERSTEIN, LOS ANGELES, CALIFORNIA,
FILMMAKER AND PHOTOGRAPHER

For those who know the essence of what an angel is, who recognize Heaven when they see it and feel it, the world is a place of magic and revelation.

Angel stories can change our lives—alter our image of "the way things are."

When we surrender to the wisdom of our angels, the Divine takes our hand and we travel sightlessly, soundlessly, wrapped in a holy vision of Perfection, on a raft of wonder, humming our own melodies of joy, gliding safely in the majesty and splendor of our greater God-tuned selves.

NOT A SCRATCH

This happened last year. My husband, George, and I were on our way home from church and I was doing my usual dozing in the car. We were making an exit going uphill on the off-ramp onto another highway when I suddenly woke up and I noticed that George was sleeping at the wheel. I said, "George!" But he was sound asleep, and so I just kept looking. The car was floating up the ramp in between the two left-turn lanes with us in the middle and at least ten cars cars on either side. It was so odd. I called him again, and I said, "George, my God!" And the car just kept going along up the ramp, and it was very, very mysterious.

It floated up the whole way, real smooth, and it came to a real soft stop. It was a long ramp, and we simply floated through. We drive an '89 LTD, which is a wide car. To get this car up the ramp between the two lanes full of cars where we're not even supposed to be, with probably ten cars on each side of us, seems totally impossible. We don't know how our car got between the lanes of cars in the first place, and how it didn't get scratched or run into anything remains a total mystery. And the car just came in at a real soft stop, like floating.

When I first looked, George was leaning back in a very relaxed way. His mouth was wide open, and his head was leaning back against the headrest. His hands were on the wheel, but just resting, because he had gone to sleep. Yet I literally had the sense that the car was being driven! You couldn't feel a motor, it didn't even feel like it was on. It just slowly proceeded very softly up the ramp. It glided. You know, you can usually feel the

tires rolling. And then it came to a real soft halt.

I was calling him in the meantime to wake up. He did wake up finally, after the car was stopped, and he said, "Mary, I think I fell asleep at the wheel." And I said, "George, I know you did!" At that point, I said, "Somebody else was driving the car!"

We looked at each other in total amazement, knowing something very strange had happened. We knew we had been protected. We really did, right away.

That's not like George, either. George is a very aggressive driver. And so I knew it was not him driving, because I was trying to wake him up as the car was floating up!

It is still mysterious to us today. How could this wide car have gotten in between two lanes of cars, with probably about ten cars on each side, and not get a scratch, nothing? When George finally woke up to see where he was, the man next to him rolled the window down and said, "Well, mister, aren't you a little close?" And George said, "Yeah, you can say that."

It was a warm feeling inside, and it was beautiful to be the one to be awakened, to be a witness to all of this. But I really do believe that "someone" else was guiding our car.

So many people say it must not have been our time, and it feels kind of special, you know, that it was not our time to go and that there is something else greater taking care of things, or something else to do. We both count that experience as a blessing.

—MARY KELLER, ST. CHARLES, MISSOURI, A DIVINE SCIENCE PRACTITIONER, WRITING ABOUT HER HUSBAND, GEORGE, A RETIRED DENTAL LABORATORY OPERATOR

Angels see through our disguises into the special, singularly pure places in our souls, which are either open or closed at any given moment, to love and to truth.

We must be willing to believe that miracles are possible in order to see the results of angels' holy presence; otherwise, we might not notice.

❖   ❖   ❖

When a miracle comes, we have earned it at some time in the past. It doesn't matter if we've forgotten. There are no accidents among angels. There is no chaos in this orderly universe.

HYDROPLANING

My daughter Kim was about eight years old, and Paige and Kelly, the twins, were still in car seats. We had just gone to order some miniblinds, and it started raining real hard. I had Kim in the front seat without a seat belt on, and I had Paige and Kelly in the back, strapped in, of course. The rain just kept falling. And before you knew it, the streets started flooding. Coming home, down the mountain by Brookfield Hospital, I started hydroplaning.

I lost control of the car. I was on top of water in a Buick Regal and I was not driving! You can't drive a car on water—the wheels won't turn! So we were flying downhill. The median in the center of the highway got covered with water. We were just sliding all over the place. I couldn't believe it…I was in the wrong dang lane! We had hydroplaned over. My daughter was screaming her head off, and I shouted, "Kim! I've lost control of the car! We're going to hit!" All of a sudden, I was on the other side of the road, and there was a car coming straight at us. There was nothing I could do. And she kept screaming, "Ahhhhh!" through the whole thing. She screamed from the top of the hill all the way down. But somehow we got to the end and nothing happened to us. Without any warning, we were on our own side of the road!

I was in the right lane again. One minute we were heading right toward another car on the wrong side of the road, and then the car was leveling off and going up again in the oncoming lane, and then we were back in our own, going right on with our trip. What happened to the oncoming car? I don't know. It just went away! It disappeared. It was wonderful. It was just the most miraculous experience. My eyes were open, but I can't even tell you what happened. I saw it, but I don't know what I saw. It did not make sense.

Something other than myself put us back in control. I just kept thanking God for a miracle. Kim will certainly remember this. It was just an absolute miracle.

It was not time for me and my three girls to go anywhere. I had to raise them to become angels.

—KAREN MADONIA, BIRMINGHAM, ALABAMA, MOTHER

Angels will not impose themselves upon people who do not want them. It's not their way. If they are not invited, they will not show up. Invite them to the party of your life. They will attend. Angels are always just outside the front door. Open it. They will be your honored guests, the life of the party.

❖   ❖   ❖

We are all much closer to the chain reaction of angel gifts and promises than we ordinarily imagine.

Angel stories remind us that God's hand really does appear occasionally to help out a regular guy.

THE COAL BUCKET

In 1974, I dropped out of college and went through the most depressing year of my life, because I had dropped out right at the beginning of the 1974 recession. It hit Colorado hard. I tried, but I couldn't even find a job at McDonald's or Burger King. After being unemployed for a number of months and moving back with Mom and Dad, I thought, "I've got to do something!" I had to borrow money from them; they had to put gas in my car so I could even look for a job. It was so depressing. I finally went up to the Great Western Sugar Factory, just outside of town in Brighton, Colorado. Sugar beets were a big industry there until about fifteen years ago. Every fall the sugar factory would employ

a thousand people. But I went out there late in the season, so almost all the jobs were already taken…and I ended up getting the worst job in the entire plant. I had to load rocks and coal into a bucket and then send them up three stories, where the bucket was tipped over and dumped into the top of a furnace. Every fifteen minutes I had to shovel the rock out of the bottom of this thing and throw it into another hopper. I did this on the graveyard shift. I hated working graveyard!

It was about my third night there. There was just myself and this one other guy, who was my boss. It was about three o'clock in the morning, and I was exhausted. We had sent a couple of buckets up, and my boss said, "Run up to the third floor and look in the window." There was a little hatch, and we had to keep the coal at just a certain level. So I ran up there, and I saw we were one bucket short of being at the correct level. So I went over to the railing, put my hands on the rail, and leaned over to yell to him to send up another bucket. Just as I leaned over the rail, I heard this little *"tick!"* As I backed up, the bucket that was already up came…*shoooo*…down! And when the bucket cleared the rail that I was leaning over, it cleared the rail by about half an inch. It would have decapitated me if I hadn't moved. I just would have been decapitated! No if, ands, or buts.

It was just a little "click," just the…the slightest brush. I collapsed on the floor and thanked God for watching over me…because I just knew! An angel must have gotten to me to move me at just the right moment or I would have been dead. I rolled on the floor and held on to myself and shook for a long, long time. I never experienced anything like that before. I've never come so close to death.

I used to work as a medical emergency technician on an ambulance. I saw people who were killed, basically, tying their shoelaces, and others who had survived when they absolutely had to have been killed, destroyed, obliterated, but who walked away without a scratch. I came away thinking, "If it's not your time, it's not your time."

It was Divine intervention. I knew instantly what had happened. I felt angels around me all the rest of that day. I never forgot it. I really felt I'd been protected.

—GREG STEVENS, NORTH HOLLYWOOD, CALIFORNIA, *LIGHT SCULPTURE ARTIST, SPECIAL EFFECTS DESIGNER, TECHNICAL WIZ*

Angels are aware of us all the time. They're able to come to us into our psyches, into our souls, into our emotions, and into our lives to help us. Sometimes they will do dramatic rescues, when we've earned it and the time is right. But inside, they are ever within our hearts' reach, within calling distance. They are loving presences that want to assist us all the time.

Being in the right place at the right time is just as possible as being in the wrong place at the wrong time. Like our friends the angels, we must be relentless in our efforts to accept goodness, to accept the infinitude of love, and to continually realign ourselves with Divine Harmony.

In day-to-day life, recognizing the simple expression of the Divine makes everything extraordinary.

What love will fortify us? An angel's love is holy and not subject to pain.

The aspiring soul can tell you about angels because he lives among them, inside his own heart.

Whenever we become like angels inside, our assignments simply come to us. We have sudden inspirations. We think of a good idea or a perfect solution and have no trouble executing it. Sometimes we receive a message that, no matter what anyone else says, we know has come from above. Because we are so attuned, regardless of how odd it may look, we feel blessed to follow it.

THE HELPING HAND

Our business fell under the devastation of the earthquake in Los Angeles. We're located right smack dab in the middle of Northridge, the epicenter of the 1994 earthquake. We have a prop shop, and about 80 percent of our stock was crushed. All the doorways from the front showroom to the back showroom were sealed closed by all the merchandise that had fallen against them, so we weren't able to enter the building.

The next day my brother-in-law, my sister, my father, and I went to the shop together. We thought we'd take a first look and try to organize. But when we got there and saw the extent of the damage to the building, we realized we should at least open up the door to let the sunshine in, because we couldn't see anything in the back rooms at all. We had no electricity.

When I say it was a disaster, I'm talking about fifteen thousand square feet of what looked like a bomb site. After a while, my father was able to pry open one of the two doors, but the other door had about twenty-five shelving panels leaning up against it, each of which weighed three hundred to five hundred pounds. My brother-in-law, Richard, and I decided that we would try to move the panels ourselves. It took both of us, two big guys, with all our strength, to physically move each one. We had about fifteen panels standing up when a tremor hit.

The tremor made the whole floor shake. The bottoms of all the panels were moving, sliding! I looked up just in time to see the panels ready to topple backward and to see Richard's head right at the point of impact. They were going to crush his head.

145

Suddenly a voice rang inside my own head, "Stop them! Try and stop them!" And the next thing I knew, my arms, with all my body weight, went up to stop these enormous weights, just long enough to delay the panels from falling, for about two seconds. It was just long enough for Richard to get his head out of the way.

Unfortunately, I was not able to get my right hand out, too, and the weight of the panels fell directly on my hand. I had seventy-five hundred pounds crush my hand. Each of the fifteen panels did, in fact, weigh over five hundred pounds. But the strangest thing happened.

I was rushed to the hospital emergency room. Amazingly, when the doctor saw the X rays, there were just two fractures. He said, "You must have had God's hand in there with yours, you must have had an angel help you, because anyone else's hand would have sustained total demolition." I realized how lucky I was and thanked God, but the doctor still told me that even with surgery, I wouldn't be able to use my hand for a year or more. He immobilized it right away, saying, "You're going to have to get used to this." But the incredible thing is, a month later, I had almost total flexibility in my fingers. I was 87 percent recovered when I should have been only 7 percent recovered.

The doctor said again, "God must have been sitting right on your shoulder." Each time the doctor said this, I felt as if angels were with me, truly protecting me, and had been with me throughout the whole experience. And they wanted me to know it. They just had the doctor mouth those words. The doctor himself had to bring up the subject of angels, because he himself was looking for a spiritual understanding of the situation. It was

146

pretty obvious there was a miracle involved.

Also, a couple of weeks after the first incident, I was a passenger in a car accident, and I automatically braced myself by putting my hands on the dashboard. We were going pretty fast and we hit quite hard. I rushed to the doctor again, who said both fractures should have been reopened, but they weren't. They were fine.

I'm a musician, and a year of inability to use my hand, in music business terms, could mean the end of a career. But in only a few weeks I was already using my pick again.

The Torah says you get rewarded ten times for the good that you do. I believe that's exactly what happened. I look at it as an example of giving somebody a hand, lending a helping hand, or showing an outstretched arm. I like to help people whenever I can. I work with people closely in a variety of capacities, and no matter what our interaction, I always do my best to do something positive for them however I can. I believe God saved my hand for me to use so I could keep giving to others.

—ALAN POLLAK, STUDIO CITY, CALIFORNIA, PROFESSIONAL MUSICIAN WITH A GOLD RECORD AND PSYCHOTHERAPIST WHO WORKS PRIVATELY AND IN HOSPITALS, PRISONS, AND STATE PROGRAMS, AND ALSO THE OWNER AND OPERATOR OF THE PROP SHOP IN NORTHRIDGE, CALIFORNIA

Whenever we appreciate and accept the divine hand of goodness, we are saved completely.

Real spirituality comes as a result of letting go. It's the

letting go that heals. Because, as it turns out, God really is good. And He is what's left over.

Our truest strength resides in our unbound nature, the uninhibited, heroic part that accepts angels and miracles, that acts for the good of the universe, regardless of outer roles, regardless of our limited thinking.

There may be earthquakes, floods, fires, tornadoes. There may be terrible scenes of evil acted out on the world movie screen....But when we are in the haven of our own love and trust in the Divine, life is filled with an infinite brand of safety and security...right up to the moment of our death.

IN THE TRENCHES

I joined the Marine Corps when I was seventeen. Shortly thereafter, I found myself in Vietnam. I arrived in late November 1967.

I was in the first battalion, 9th Marines, and the name of our unit, believe it or not, was the Ghost Battalion. We were also known as Charcoal Charlie and the Walking Dead; those were some of the names that were given to us because of the skirmishes we had survived through.

We were in Khe Sanh. Most people have heard of it, because there was a huge battle there. It was called the Siege of

Khe Sanh. It was a very important battle, and it received a tremendous amount of press.

My unit was on the north perimeter of that air base. There were probably several thousand people with various support activities, hundreds of ground troops, all to watch the perimeter. In January of '68 we dug in. We created a very elaborate trench system, with many rows of barbed-wire fence, trip wire in all kinds of patterns, and land mines, too, between us and the outer perimeter. Planes wouldn't actually fly into the base. They air-dropped food and supplies. No one could land because there was so much incoming artillery. We were constantly under a barrage of some sort or another. Immediately in front of me was a huge open zone where they did these drops.

There was one guy in my platoon, Mike Lopez, who was my lookout alternate. We'd switch watches with each other. He shared my bunk. One night in March, our platoon was given the assignment to be the lookouts for that evening. There were three posts broken up into groups of four. I was in charge of one group, Mike was in charge of another, and another guy headed the third. My group was still inside the very last string of wires, so we had some barrier between us and the open space. The other two lookout posts were outside the wire. We had strung out ammo cans with spent brass (used shells loaded with high explosives) and ran a detonation cord up to our command post. We also had a fifty-five-gallon drum of jet fuel with det cord around that. So we put up as many defenses as we possibly could, beyond what the Marine Corps allowed us to do. We were told that we were supposed...we were gonna slow 'um down.... We weren't gonna stop anybody. We were supposed to be overrun in

the case of a major offensive. So that's what we had to look forward to on a day-to-day basis, you know? Didn't know when it was comin' or if it was comin'!

This one evening, it was fairly quiet, like any of the nights we had spent there previously for two months. This particular night, one of the units claimed that they had some activity. Everybody had a radio, each little group had its own. All of a sudden, around midnight, some gunfire started going off. There was shooting back and forth. It was not around the four of us, it was one hundred yards away. Then somewhere in that racket there was an explosion. Shortly thereafter, I could have sworn I saw somebody coming through the fence to my left. The three of us just opened up fire in that direction. We looked to see if there was anything else coming at us, and then we got orders to come on in, inside the main wire and back to the main position.

Then there was another major explosion, all kinds of gunfire going off. I told my guys to head on in and I'd pick up the tail. We had to follow a certain path because of the way the barbed-wire was set up. As I was running in, there was gunfire coming from our perimeter, shooting out, which they shouldn't have been doing because there was fire coming back in and we didn't know where it was coming from or who it was coming from.

At one point, my guys got ahead of me as I was getting ready to go over this tree stump. A hand came on my back and pushed me down. It was Mike Lopez. He said, "Get down!" and I hit the dirt. But as I was goin' down, I heard bullets whizzing by my head. They were right there. You could hear 'em sing. After I hit the deck, Mike said, "Get up! Let's go!" and I started hauling my butt in. I heard him, I felt him....He had pushed me into the trench. I knew his voice. I knew his accent.

When I came in somebody said, "Is there anybody else?" And I said, "Yeah, Mike's right behind me." I got in the trench. I argued with everyone that Mike was right behind me, but we waited for somebody else to get in, and no one else came in. Within about two hours, I went back out and I found Mike. He had lost both of his legs above his knees, and he had many fragments that had gone through his body. I carried him in that evening. I put him in his bag and zipped it up, carried him in personally, and I'm tellin' ya, I couldn't believe it. He was *outside* the wire, a good twenty-five yards from the wire and a good hundred yards from where he pushed me down. Ya know, *no legs!* It was *impossible!* It's not possible that he would have come to me and then run back out there. No way. Because it was one of those two explosions that had taken him out.

None of that made any sense to me. I think I was definitely saved by...something obviously good—and as impossible as it seems, it happened. It was back when nobody believed anything. You don't want everyone, your peers, to think you're off your rocker....Back in the late sixties there is no way you could have talked about it, especially with all the drugs going on. Everybody would have shrugged it off.

But something or someone—Mike himself or my guardian angel—saved my life that night. That I know. Someone was watching over me in the trenches.

Actually, I never mentioned this story to anyone. It was kind of eerie. I was pretty numb to everything, it was so surrealistic. When somebody is dead, they're gone. You just move on to the next situation. You really can't dwell on that sort of thing.

And there's something about being eighteen years old that tells me, now that I look back at it more than twenty-five years later, that something else, something *else* took place. I mean, these are the feelings I have today I never had then.

There are a lot of instances where you just watch things happen around you that seem unbelievable. When we thought about home, back then, home was like a fairy tale. It was dreamland. It's pretty primal.

You get to eat, you hunt, and you sleep, but mostly you're the predator and you're out there hunting and sleeping, and the only reason you're doin' that is so you can eat. It got pretty basic. I have a strong understanding of why young countries such as Lebanon, and these guys over in Bosnia, are fighting all the time. I mean it's real simple. There's no challenge. These guys forget what life is really all about. Fighting is the easy way out. There's no thinking involved. It's very basic. That's too bad.

It's a story I think of, not too often but often enough. And I know that there's a reason that I made that trip back from Vietnam. I can't say twenty-five years later that I have made a visible impact on the world as I know it, but maybe I've had an impact on someone else's life who will make an impact. Maybe just telling this story will help someone have a little more faith. I'm sure I tried to tell someone, but it just seems that I never got the story out, till now. I feel good telling it. I have needed to. Because it happened, and it was a miracle.

—Martin Charles Cottrell, Redondo Beach, California,
Beverly Hills Porsche salesman

In this life we are independent, yet we are interconnected. We must surrender and yet take responsibility. We are each unlimited in essence, yet we have divine friends who watch over us. Death is a part of our evolution and destiny, yet sometimes angels rescue a select few from it temporarily. Why the paradoxes and the confusion? To the angels, there are no paradoxes. All is perfect.

We have to bypass or wholly transcend the mind to gain any real understanding. Our mind goes quiet at certain angel thoughts and experiences, and that is where our answer is. In the silence. In silence and stillness there is only experience of oneness and knowing.

The hand of God reaches down to assist us, through warning, through grace, through inspiration, through love. An angel story is an expression of universal caring.

Sometimes they come in heavenly garb and sometimes pedestrian. Their wings may appear as gossamer or feathery, showered in blue or gold or whitest light. Their halos may be a crown of stars, a simple glow, or an inner illumination.

But then again, they may look like a mailman, a beggar, a doctor, a child, or even an animal. How can we identify them? Perhaps not till later. When we know their visit wasn't of the ordinary kind, and their influence, so special.

THE SKIER

I've never told anyone this story before. But it's true.

A few years ago, I was skiing. I skied often. I was on a very steep slope when I got separated from my friends. I was suddenly alone, barreling down the hill much too fast for my own good, zooming directly toward some trees. Unable to change course or stop myself, I realized that I was about to crash. The trees were growing taller by the second. But in another instant, I was stopped…still…and everything was silent.

I had been stopped by something, but I hadn't crashed and I didn't lose consciousness. I felt only a thud, and then someone was helping me sit to up. When I looked up, there was a tall man dressed all in black with a black ski cap. He stood directly in front of me, with his brilliant, lovely blue eyes looking into mine, and he had his hands on my shoulders. I'll never forget what he said, or the beautiful flutelike sound of his voice. "You're going to be all right. Don't worry," he said. I closed my eyes to relax for a second and take a deep breath. When I opened them again, he was gone. I looked all around and there were no footprints in the snow. I knew immediately that he was my guardian angel.

—INVESTMENT BROKER, LOS ANGELES, CALIFORNIA, NAME WITHHELD

Perhaps we will never know that they really were angels. It may never occur to us to think further. But we will find some-

154

thing new by remembering the magnificent soul looking out from those gentle and friendly eyes.

That is why it behooves you to really look when you look into the eyes of others. Make an effort to see people in their entirety, as they really are.

Give credit to greatness of heart, of spirit, of courage, of mildness, or of freedom you may see in even the roughest exterior or the smallest frame. Accept the gifts emanating from their eyes, their personalities, or simply the aura they carry with them as they pass, and let it touch yours.

HEALINGS

The art of love is an angel's art. Enter into this sacred art, and the world becomes exquisite.

Watching over us…traveling with us…standing by us…angels are beings who know our deepest hearts…can hear our thoughts…feel our longings…and understand.

156

DAKOTA'S ANGEL

Ever since my son Dakota was born and had to be placed in the infant intensive care unit, I have always been extra worried whenever he gets any illnesses or even a cold. One night when he was about four months old, he was having an extremely hard time getting to sleep. He had a severe ear infection and a slight fever. I wasn't feeling well myself, and I remember how long the night felt, what with him waking up every few minutes and crying.

I remember feeling so tired, so incredibly tired, and thinking to myself, "How am I going to get through this night?" My husband wasn't home, so I put Dakota in our bed with me. I held him and prayed that he would be all right and feeling better in the morning...if we could just get to the morning.

I had already given Dakota his medicine, yet he seemed to be getting worse, drifting in and out of sleep. I remember just lying there looking at him. Then I prayed. I remember asking for God to "send an angel down for Dakota, send someone who can put their hand on his body and let him sleep in comfort."

After a matter of seconds, I looked up, and there, sitting on the end of the bed, was this vision. It was a little girl! It was a little blond girl with the fairest complexion. I knew I couldn't be dreaming because I had just said my prayers. I looked at this face, this beautiful face, and she smiled at me. I immediately realized she was there for Dakota's sake. She was giving me the feeling that it was okay for me to fall asleep now, that she would take over and watch out for him through the night.

I fell asleep. Dakota fell asleep. The next morning he was

fine. He had gotten some rest, and I rejoiced in what I can only call a miracle. Once again in my life, I feel blessed to have received another affirmation of my beliefs and my prayers. Many people I tell this story to tell me I must have been only dreaming. Fair enough, I suppose. However, I know in my heart that I was nowhere near dreaming. I feel sure that the little girl who came to Dakota that night is truly one of his angels.

I cannot wait for the day I can tell him about her. Better yet, if he ever tells me about her, I will listen, and I will believe.

—JENNIFER MILLWEE, VAN NUYS, CALIFORNIA

Little children, most recently having come to earth, are still delicious little slices of Heaven themselves, naturally protected.

When the innocent, like children, suffer, if we know our angels, we can trust that God is taking care of our little and defenseless ones, too.

Angels appear in different forms and shapes to different people at different times. The possibilities of disguise are endless. They are infinitely creative.

Sometimes the stories that people tell of their encounters with angels are those of invisible forces. Sometimes, however, they are more personalized.

Visiting mankind for eons, angels' visits are of a specific nature and yet are somewhat difficult to define in words. Described as "light"—exquisite, peaceful—angels do not haunt, nor are they uninvited visitors with hidden agendas. They are not aliens from other worlds or disembodied spirits after their own rewards. Angels are God's helpers, our compassionate guides, anonymous rescuers, but above all, implacable friends, messengers of hope and inspiration.

When angels make contact, we are assured. It is a deep connection, no matter how superficial the scene.

VIETNAM VET

I was in a VA hospital in Portland, back in 1977 or '78. I had an experience, and it was really freaky. I haven't exactly talked about it before today.

I remember I was asking some questions because I was in Vietnam and I had both my legs blown out from underneath me. My biggest question was: Is God always there? I had listened to a radio program, and there was a pastor on who said, "If you have any questions about your eternal salvation, pray to God so that you can move heaven and earth to get you the answers." And I did that. The next week, a pastor came to the hospital. Through him, I came to the Lord, along with another two fellas.

To get to the story, as a friend and I were walking in front of the hospital—it was about eight-fifteen at night—this girl came

right up to us. She was blond, wearing overalls. She had been crying. She said, "My brother is dying. He's not going to be here too long!" She asked us to pray for him, to go in and see him, because she couldn't. She also told us that he was an atheist; he didn't believe in Christ, he didn't believe in salvation, he didn't believe in eternal life or anything else.

She gave us the room number, and we went in there. The nurse had just gotten done taking blood samples. He had leukemia and throat cancer—they had just finished operating on him. He was in bad shape. The doctor came in and told us that the guy'd be dead in the morning.

When a pastor came in moments later, he asked him, "Would you like to have salvation? Do you know the condition you're in?" And he nodded his head yes. He could hardly talk. So we all kinda prayed around his bed.

The next morning, my friend and I went back. I went into his room expecting to find him dead. We saw his bed was cleaned out and the mattress was rolled up and everything. We asked the staff if he was still alive, and they said "Yes," but he had to be transferred outa there.

About three months later I met the same guy in a hallway and, believe it or not, he was passing out flyers for the chaplain's office. He ran right up to me, recognized me right off the bat, and I recognized him. The scar on his throat was just practically gone. He said, "I want to know how you guys got up to my room when you came in to pray for me, because no one in the chaplain's service here remembers!" And I said, "Well, this girl outside came out of nowhere, and she asked us to." He said, "I want to know more about this girl. Who was she?" And I said, "Well, it was just this girl. She wanted to make sure that you were going to make it through the night. She was really afraid that, ya know, you were gonna be lost." And he said, "What did she say her name was?" And I said, "I remember her saying that she was your sister."

His face just went cold white; you had to have been there. He just dropped everything he had in his hands. And then he looked at me and said, "My sister's dead! She was killed in a car wreck three years ago!" And he pulled out his wallet to show me a picture…and it was the same girl! It was the very same girl! There was no question. I don't know if she was as pretty-lookin' in that picture, but it was the same girl—she was even wearing the same clothes! It just totally blew my mind. I rocked back in my chair. I couldn't even think. I was stunned. I was just sitting there alone, going, "What in the heck is going on here?" I never experienced anything like that before, and I'll tell ya, it put a whole new meaning into faith and belief for me. Every time I think about it…I can't reason it away.

—AS TOLD TO THE AUTHOR IN A RADIO INTERVIEW

It is the unprotected soul, whether by birth or by choice, whether by courage or humility, whether by catastrophe or inner glory, it is the vulnerable one who attracts the angels best.

When we accept angels in our lives, we can accept that our loved ones who have passed on have not simply disappeared but have joined the heavenly forces and have angelic protection of their own.

Sometimes God is too big a concept to deal with, but an angel always fits just right.

❖ ❖ ❖

When we are confused by life, feeling empty and out of sync, it is reassuring to know there are beings who are always in harmony, in a state of heavenly grace, knowing that we are momentarily lost, willing to extend their support for just that moment so that we can relax and find our way again.

Sometimes lavishing us with praise and encouragement, sometimes instructional or even stern, the angels may urge us ahead or warn us to slow down, grab hold of what little courage we have and lift us up, shower us with Divine acceptance or scold us and order us to stop or let go.

The angels teach freedom. They promote love. When we ask for guidance in these subjects, we always get the highest, and when we persist, we are graced with revelation.

THE BALCONY

My husband and I were having a lot of marriage problems in Germany, twelve years ago. I really didn't know it, but he was having an affair. He would not communicate with me; he would avoid any situation where we would be alone. It got to the point

where he would walk out of the room if I wanted to talk. I knew something was very wrong in the marriage, but I couldn't get him to sit down. He was always too busy. It was really bad. But we had plans for a long time and tickets to go to Mexico for a vacation in Puerto Vallerta and Guadalajara, so we finally went away together.

There is a beautiful church there where people pray, and they actually leave their crutches and their wheelchairs. Many people have been healed. Larry's Jewish, and I'm Christian, but he went with me because it was part of the tour. So I went to the altar and I prayed, asking God to give me some aid. "I don't know what You can do, Lord. Can You send one of Your angels and arrange for me to have some time to talk to him? That's all I need. Maybe I can straighten it out. Please help me to at least communicate with my husband." So far, throughout the trip, on the airplane he would say, "I'm tired," and in the hotel he would be reading. At meals he was preoccupied.

But we got to Puerto Vallerta, and we had a beautiful hotel with a room on the highest floor. And I said, "Lord, arrange it this time so that he will not be able to run away." And I even said, "You have sent me an angel before. Maybe You could arrange to have an angel sent to me this time, too."

Even in Puerto Vallerta, Larry would say, "Now, I am going to the beach," "I'm hungry," or "I'm going to take a nap." He would just always have an excuse. This went on all day. Then, the second morning I woke up, it was very, very early, must have been only four-thirty in the morning. And the bed was empty. Larry had gone out on the balcony. I guess he had so many guilt problems, he also couldn't sleep very well. So I went out on the

balcony with him, and I thought, "Oh, maybe I can talk to him now." So I went out there, and he was sitting, and I said, "So, Larry, we have got to talk. What's wrong?" And he said, "There's nothing wrong. I'm going back to sleep!"

He tried to go back in, but the door would not open up. The door had locked! We were sitting there for three hours. That door would not open! I swear to God! We couldn't do a thing about it. We had to wait until seven o'clock, when people started finally appearing and there was activity. Even then, we were so high up that they couldn't hear us. Larry would scream down, but they wouldn't hear. Nobody could hear us. So for three hours I could say anything I wanted to, and he had no way to get away from me! He had two choices: to jump down from the twenty-third floor or stay.

Finally, around eight o'clock or so, someone heard us down there, looked up, and saw us waving hands…and they tried to find us. I heard people going from door to door, saying, "Are you the ones?" When they didn't get any answer elsewhere, they figured it must be us. So they opened the door and came into our room. By that time the manager was there. But they couldn't open the balcony door, either. So they had a mechanic come up, and he opened it. The manager assured us that this had never happened before. He was very apologetic. They gave us a free dinner. What had happened was that the door actually locked itself. The manager couldn't understand what was going on, because *there was no lock*. The door to the balcony had *no lock*.

When I was alone with my husband, everything came out. It was only the beginning. He told me later that after that talk things were finally set into motion for him to come to terms

with the situation, and our marriage was saved.

My request was very specific. I mean, I know now that God has a real sense of humor. I wanted time alone, and God locked the door.

I believe you have to ask for help. God loves each one of us, like you are the only child. Each one of us is loved totally and completely, nobody is loved more than another, but it's a love that is incredible. I wish everyone knew that they are never alone. That always help is around you. And He does send His angels. I really do believe that.

—BRIDGET NEWTON, LAS VEGAS, NEVADA,
RESERVATIONS CLERK AT BALLY'S HOTEL

Sometimes, when we are not telling the truth, we block the angelic, heavenly power that wants to flow through us from correcting our life picture.

If you use the information at your disposal, with honesty and goodwill toward all, the angels will assist you.

When we realign ourselves with the truth by releasing the bitter or fearful, vengeful or prideful feelings, we return to our natural states of courage, acceptance, and peace. We begin to take actions toward our freedom, and we thrive again, seeking good, and finding it like angels.

Awareness of angels doesn't dismiss the responsibility we

have for ourselves; it opens the door to our greater friends and holier influences.

Angel stories prove that all is forgiven.

Angels are affirmations of life, guardians of hope and well-being.

It is apparently not God's will that we live forever. But when we live on the side of the angels, we somehow reap a little more protection, a sense of unfailing companionship even as we approach the end.

Angel encounters provide planetary nourishment of the celestial kind. Sharing our stories with one another will help reduce our psychic burden and will help to alleviate many levels of suffering.

NEAR DEATH

My name is Ricci and I am eleven years old. When I was two, I had a near-death experience. I was out in the garage helping my mother do the laundry. My sisters, Jodie and Sara, were in the house cleaning their rooms, while my father was working on his car. I had gotten bored helping my mother, so I decided to go out in the backyard and ride my tricycle around the pool. I started going faster and faster, and my training wheel got caught on the edge of the pool. I landed in the pool, and I didn't know how to swim.

I blacked out for a minute and then woke up to find myself in a huge, bright bricked tunnel with a very bright white light at the end. I was very scared and didn't move. Then I heard a calm, comforting, soft-spoken voice say, "Don't be afraid. I will guide you." After I heard the voice, I turned around and saw a big angel. She said to me, "I am your guardian angel. I will guide you and keep you safe."

She held out her hand, and I quickly grabbed it. We started to walk down the tunnel. When we reached the end, she turned to me and asked, "Would you like to enter the light or go back?" I answered, "I would like to go back. I'm scared." Once again I blacked out. My mother found me and called 911. I was flown to Loma Linda, where I was diagnosed with no chance of survival. Five days later I was fine and released.

I never really remembered my trip to the tunnel until a couple of years ago when I saw a picture of an angel that looked just like my angel. We were in a bookstore, and I started pulling on my mother's hand saying, "Mommy, Mommy, that's my angel!" That's when I told her the story of the tunnel. She believed me right away. We talk about angels all the time now. I believe in angels more than ever.

—RICCI ENRIQUEZ, BARSTOW, CALIFORNIA, A SEVENTH-GRADE STUDENT
AT KENNEDY MIDDLE SCHOOL

The answers angels offer ride in a voice of superior clarity, travel in a sheer cloud of vulnerability and a breathtaking kind of love.

To the attentive soul, the afterglow of silence reiterates a million times the point we most forget: "Be still and know that I am God."

Know you don't have to die to experience angels. You don't have to have a near-death experience to see the light and know you're safe and loved by the Divine.

Angels remind us of a greater destiny meant for the soul.

We are found by our heavenly angels among the leftover pieces of our half-delivered love. To build our castle to the stars it's best to send the rest complete with envelope addressed or not and let the angels carry it to God. And let Him find you then, to thank you with a kiss. God never loses those who give.

The angels ask that you take yourself to places inside where you can be happy before your time is gone and you have lost your way—or worse, your heart. Be gentle with people and feel the one authentic Greatness. You cannot mistake it or misplace it, for it is everywhere. To an angel there is no experience mightier than this knowledge.

BY THE POOL

M y parents were getting our house exterminated, so we went to my Aunt Mary's house in Santa Fe Springs. I was in her Jacuzzi that evening enjoying the air when I felt something behind me. The whole weekend I kept feeling the presence of something around me very strongly, and I kept hearing the word "guardian." I was a little frightened by the experience, especially after I went to bed and kept getting these sort of flash visions, where I would see a lighted being with wings by the poolside.

Not long afterward, I was back at my Aunt Mary's with my boyfriend, and I said, "Honey, would you walk with me by the poolside, because I've got to find something out. It's driving me nuts." And as we went by the pool, the wind started to whip up wildly around me, and I felt as if something had entered inside me or that I had walked right into something. I asked my boyfriend if he felt anything, and he said, "No, I don't. I think this is something for you to feel."

Then that night when I went to bed, I saw these enormous angels. I was going to sleep and I had another flash vision, and all of a sudden I saw these enormous angels in my consciousness. It was like a flash picture. They were absolutely beautiful.

When I came home after my first experience, I asked for a sign. I heard them tell me, "We are not outside you, we are inside you. You must remember that, because you may come back here and not feel the experience again."

The most important thing about angels is, they will give you messages all day long. I'll be watching TV and feeling bad, say, about my weight, and all of a sudden on the television, there's an angel. And it happens almost every single day.

Angels are the simplest things to connect with. You'll find them in any place of innocence. And if you realize that everything is innocent, you realize the universe is safe. So wherever love is, they are. So they must be everywhere.

—KATHERINE SCORZO, BELL, CALIFORNIA, ARTIST AND WRITER

An angel is gladness and good thinking. It is rich surprise and happy answers all at once. It is melting into yourself when you are crying uncontrollable tears of joy and you don't know why.

An angel is like meeting yourself for the very first time. Like facing a part of your heart you have forgotten and claiming it, saying, "Yes, you are mine."

Know your angels in your precious self, in secret passages of your own longings for the light you treasure most and kiss when no one sees, and call your own.

We must build our own bridges to the angels. Every loving thought, every giving act, every wholesome intention is part of the construction. As Heaven would have it, when we start building our stairway to Heaven, the stairway takes on magical properties of its own. One day it begins to carry us to Heaven....Not climbing anymore, we find ourselves falling up the Divine staircase, and we can fly!

❖ ❖ ❖

Whenever we let go, we create a window through which the angels and all the love in the universe instantly flow.

The Runner

I used to be a runner in New York. I used to feel that there were angels with me, running with me, carrying me. I never remember hearing my feet touch the ground when I ran. It was like the only time I ever felt free.

—Stanley Newton, Venice, California,
professional photographer

On silent, fledgling wings the silent mind wanders toward infinity and gets lost among the angels.

❖ ❖ ❖

My heart steadies, touching Yours. My hands open, holding Yours. My mind quiets, hearing Yours. Your grace surrounds me, for I am Yours. We cannot fly away, for anywhere we go is Heaven.

ME-MOM

About six years ago, my grandmother died after a fairly safe and routine surgery. She was young and healthy, and died a week after the surgery because of an infection. We were devastated that God took her without warning. A few weeks after her death, I was resting in my Center City apartment. I was sleeping lightly, or twilighting, you might say, fully aware of my surroundings. I was definitely not dreaming. Gently I felt my right arm rise off the bed from my side. It was suspended as a warm, small hand grasped my hand and gently held it. This lasted for about thirty seconds. Then the hand let go of mine and my arm drifted back down. It was without a doubt my grandmother comforting me.

Several weeks after that incident, I had a very vivid and special dream. I was in a field with flowers and animals. My grandmother came to me, smiling and radiant, looking beautiful. I said, "Me-Mom, how come you don't visit me more? I have missed you." She smiled and said, "I am always near you, although you may not realize it." She pointed to a squirrel in the tree and a butterfly fluttering around me. I realized that she would always be guarding me, protecting me from harm. I haven't dreamt about her lately, but I often feel her near me. I do have angels around me!

—KIM M. DiGIACOMO, D.P.M., F.A.C.F.S., DIPLOMATE—AMERICAN
BOARD OF PODIATRIC SURGERY, LANGHORNE, PENNSYLVANIA

When a deceased relative, friend, or lover, someone who has been an angel for us on earth, comes in a vision or in a dream and makes his or her invisible presence known, profound healing takes place that wipes away decades-old burdens of grief, fear, and bitterness.

Just the sight or presence of that most important loved one is the perfect medicine for so many ailments. No winged vision of Divine Love could replace the value and meaning of the sight of that one face or the sound of that one voice, the realization of that one all-important person being with us again for a moment, to know that they are watching over us—and still care.

The angels play, fearing nothing, owning everything, galloping, cascading, streaming, billowing, dancing within God.

Applauding the pea and the strawberry, the willow and the bee. Engaging the whale in holy discourse. Dreaming colorful universes within the sunlight. Tiptoeing across the star-pinned heavens out of sight. Shaking hands with every tree and butterfly. Parading through the petals of every cheery flower. Skipping like stones across the wind, glory-bound. Changing shapes in mountain shadows. Bristling and diving unannounced between chilly ocean waves and white-capped tips. They are everywhere.

Our angels embrace us when with courage we step out into the unknown place where wishes are not merely fantasies but

174

fates, where dreams don't represent ignorance but intelligence, where the heart melts because it suddenly has what it needs—all it needs—and can accept itself as a perfect piece of the mysterious heart of God.

Attuning ourselves with angels, we come to know our deep, abiding connection to love, become aware of our inner eternal power, our ageless permission to win, and an ocean inside us of borderless joy.

THE BIKE RIDE

My angel experience happened this year in May when I participated in the California AIDS Ride, which was a bicycle ride from San Francisco to Los Angeles, around five hundred miles. We raised over 1.6 million dollars. There were four hundred and sixty of us who participated.

I had never been involved in charities or organizations before. I've always been kind of busy with other things. I was a little nervous about it. First of all, the athletic part was awesome, and then dealing with all the different people.

When I left San Francisco that morning, it was very cold. It was a typical San Francisco morning, you know, on the verge of drizzling. And I thought, "Oh, God, what did I get myself into?" Throughout the day we had "support and gear" stops about every fifteen miles. After lunch, which is the third stop, I was feeling pretty good. No problems. But I realized I was only halfway

through the day. I still had a long way to go, and I was already pretty tired. But this was when I had my angel experience.

When I left after lunch, it was kind of stormy along the coast and there were a lot of clouds rolling; it looked like it was going to start raining. Suddenly I felt as though I was energized and that pedaling my bike was not a problem. It was almost like I wasn't there. I don't know if my mind had just shut off, but I was just going for it. There was no soreness, there was no tiredness, and my speed was picking up more and more, and I thought, "Well, maybe I got a good tail wind or something like that." So I didn't stop at the next two stops. I went straight from lunch all the way in to camp. It felt as though someone was with me.

It was effortless. It felt like there was a hand on the back of my bike seat and then behind that hand other people or spirits, you know, also pushing it, not only in a physical sense, but in a spiritual sense, too. And I just flew.

I know what sports highs are, because I'm very athletic. Adrenaline had nothing to do with it. It felt like there was a spirit behind me that had his hand on the back of my seat pushing my bike the whole way. I felt like I was literally being pushed. I flew by each stop. I just kept going. And I didn't even realize they were there until I got into camp.

The biggest thing about this experience for me was that I literally felt the spirits of all these people who have passed— there can't be that many people that pass for no reason—I felt that this collective group of spirits came up behind me physically and spiritually, and basically helped me through the rest of that day. Just that one day. From lunch on, I don't remember seeing another rider, and I didn't talk to anyone else. I don't

remember passing people. When I got into camp that night, I snapped out of it. I even turned around and looked behind me to see if these people, this group of spirits, were really there.

I feel like all the people who have passed away because of this disease, that their spirits are still just as strong and as powerful as ever. There was peace, a serenity involved…there was joy. I knew that ride was nothing compared with the suffering that so many people have been through. Somehow I felt that it wasn't just my duty after that, but it was now in my heart. My company has donated a lot of things to the organization since that day. The Jeffrey Goodman Center works a lot with corporate sponsors, and lots of times we need to send things. So my company, Box Brothers, will send those items, you know, ship 'em and pack 'em for free, and stuff like that. This experience allowed me to do a lot of good things for a lot of different people.

But most important, there's the spirit inside me that really felt helped to help. That's where the biggest miracle took place, I think. My friends were shocked at the change in me. I encourage them to be charitable, too, now. I've always been an overachiever. I was a diver when I was a kid. I dove on a national level but I never felt that I had accomplished anything. Even owning my own successful business didn't ever feel like an accomplishment to me. But when I stepped off the bike in L.A. I felt like I had accomplished some-thing. For the first time in my life. And that was a wild feeling.

That one afternoon, I just flew the whole way. It changed me. I thought I was just goin' on a bike ride.

—MATHEW TAPSCOTT, LOS ANGELES, CALIFORNIA, OWNER OF
BOX BROTHERS, A PACKAGING AND SHIPPING STORE

The more effortless our soaring, the more our angels come to us. In sport or art, in passion or the solitude of silence, they catch us in the final inch, the endless burst, the open throttled *"whoosh!"*...when we let go.

Angel experiences help explain the mysterious and give us greater courage to go on.

Angel stories prove just how close our Source, our connection, our holy mentors are.

The angels tell us that courage takes us Home. No weak ones walk the distance to the Infinite. Every test must be met within oneself, every leaf upturned and rock looked under; no hidden meanings or agendas are accepted, no shadows of our former selves are housed, and broken hearts will not be allowed.

Keep your eye on the target, but shoot for the moon. For Heaven is where you will find the answers that you cannot find on earth. Go gently through the world and find the simplicity of your power. Mark your days with warmth and true inspiration.

Find the meaning of your life by revealing who you are. Remember...you are what angels sing about. Your presence in this world can make Heaven applaud. Take all the support you are given. You deserve it. You're on your way.

Is it truly possible to climb beyond ourselves into blissful realities that expand and grow forever? It is our human right to face joy, to dive in…to find a place inside ourselves that transcends everything physical, everything "known." Rapture, bliss, ecstasy, Heaven, Nirvana, enlightenment. Poets have written about it. Saints of all religions know these places that may be reached within the human soul. They know about the holy forces. They know about angels.

When the soul is filled with light, it does not matter if one is on a throne or a pulpit or on a bed of straw, if one's body is strong or dying, if one is in the company of millions or alone in a room, if one is in the wilds of nature or in an empty dungeon, in motion or at rest, clothed or naked, with food or without. The ecstasy of Heaven is felt not in the outer senses but the inner ones.

The soul, the body, and the brain instantly know the rejuvenating effects of the flow of divine energy in the spiritual heart. Opening our heart is a path that all religions ask us to follow. The inner disciplines that give rise to flight are then easily mastered when the soul has set itself on fire for love of the Divine.

THE YOGA TEACHER

I was doing a yoga breathing exercise, quite a difficult one, which, done correctly, produces an altered state. I did it for a very long time until, suddenly, I slipped out of my body and rose up above it. I was floating above my body, looking down, when I noticed that I wasn't alone.

I noticed that there was a presence. I really don't know how to describe it in words because it really does an injustice to use words. It was light...like a light, with me, near me, a feeling of very profound love, just in every direction. That was just its state, and I happened to be there. It wasn't like "I'm giving it to you"...there wasn't anything particular like that. It was just love, and in this love, it was very warm, very loving.

This so-called location that I was in really had no boundaries, so it's hard to talk about it in linear terms. It was just a single presence, and I was part of it. It wasn't like it was separate from me. It wasn't like I was here and there was an angel out there. It was just all one presence. Let's put it that way.

I communicated with it mentally, without speaking. And the dialogue was effortless. The presence said, "Do you see your body down there?" "Yes," I answered. It said, "Do you want to go back?" And I looked at it, and I said, "Well, it's a nice body. It's young, it's healthy. I don't mind, it's nice." Then it said, "You can go back or you can go on." The spirit continued talking, and I thought for a second. Then I said, "Well, will you still be here if I go back?" It said, "Yes." So I said, "Okay, I'll go back." As soon as I said that, wham, slam, back in the body. It felt like

putting your foot in a shoe that was three sizes too small. Maybe a hundred sizes too small.

To go from the immensity of that bliss and then to be jammed back in the tiny, limited body was shocking. Still, the residue of that experience and the fragrance of it lasted for weeks. It was very powerful.

But gradually it faded, as experiences have a tendency to do. But that energy, that presence I visited, was very real. And I didn't project anything onto it. I didn't project a name. I didn't call it an angel or a being or a guide. I'm not into that. It was just a presence, unnamed. That was nice. I liked it. That presence is always, always there.

—YOGA TEACHER IN SANTA MONICA, CALIFORNIA, NAME WITHHELD

More and more people are looking inside for the sustenance there seems to be a shortage of in the world—love, peace, happiness, fulfillment.

It's time for us to surrender our hearts, to cross into the glorious territory of Being—the final frontier. Like our angels, in the inner invisible realms we will find what we need.

Meditation and prayer are peaceful experiences that help us feel the divine energy literally coming into our bodies, into our minds and our hearts. Though this energy is always in us, we suddenly become aware of it.

When we identify with the Spirit within us, we know in our essence that we, too, have this same freedom that resolves all paradoxes of life effortlessly; we become the whole being that we are, fully embraced by the Divine.

When you're feeling the kind of inner peace that comes directly from Heaven, then all the cares and the worries of the world melt away. The issue of security disappears. You know you're 100 percent okay now, that you have always been fully protected and always will be. There's no comparison between that feeling and the idea that you can manipulate your life to avoid catastrophes and try to one-up other people by being "smarter."

Angels are superior in the ways of love, ever urging us to rise into the divine light of their presence.

Let go of your fears and yearnings as you have never let go before. The angels' essence will surround you. They will stay with you as long as you like…forever, really.

We will find the angels threading evanescence through a trillion empty, love-attracting thoughts, dropping hope between the sad imaginings of a billion shattered dreams, striking harmony notes like bells of joy in the vast, beatific inner reaches of our tenderest God-blessed hearts.

Great souls have always found new doorways, new pathways through the world, places where one can walk inside oneself, so that the feet never touch the ground and the being is never soiled.

In faith, we fill in the blanks of our hearts with breathless, breathtaking love. What Heaven offers the faithful is always superior to our thinking and will always improve our state of mind…and usually our lives as well.

Because the fancy dances of our mental flights have turned us from ourselves, the angels cannot catch our eye, and only when we come again into the sacred chambers of our hearts will they reveal themselves.

THE HEAVENLY VOICE

I'm an architect. I had just ended the most serious relationship of my life, and I was feeling a little lost. I knew I needed assistance and direction at that time. And I'd been asking for it.

I keep a journal. At the head of the week, I usually write something positive like an affirmation of what I want to happen that week. This one day I wrote down: "Angels, assist me!" I wanted an assist or some help, some encouragement. You know, life sometimes is a struggle for just so damn long. And you're tired of this crap and you think, "When am I going to get some results here?"

So one night that week, I'm sleeping in my bed at home in Santa Barbara. This voice wakes me up, a very strong, firm, clear voice. A woman's voice says, "Bill, Bill." It's still dark, and I'm startled, so I wake up. I think, "Wow." I look around and I realize it's not a dream. There is definitely something here. I was looking slightly up, and there was a long, tall figure, sort of like drapery. I didn't see much body detail or anything, just a lot of light. In some ways it's kind of like concentric rings—like when you throw rocks in a pond—rings coming out of the head. And there were no clear facial features. There seemed to be two or maybe more. I knew they represented infinities. I felt they were my spirit guides.

So I say, "Who is it? Who *is* this?" I don't get a clear answer. Whatever the answer is, it's something like "Your protectors, your allies...your angels. We've been with you always."

I recognized that most of my life, way over 99 percent of my

185

life, I've been unaware of these friends of mine, but they knew everything that has gone on in my life. Every moment, you know—suffering, joy, and everything else. And they were completely loving toward me. In a way I felt like they were a part of me that I wasn't paying attention to.

Well, that night I had a dialogue with them for the first time. I'm lying down, with my head on the pillow, kind of tilted toward my feet. So I'm looking up, at about thirty-five degrees. They were standing at the head of my bed. This was not a dream or just imaginary energy, this was like "Wow! Who *are* you?" I felt really lucky. I had finally made contact with my own guardian angels. The feeling of finally seeing and hearing these beings of light was like when something's right on the tip of your tongue but you can't remember the word, or trying to remember a dream but it's just over the edge, so you can't. I knew them, but I had never met them like this, that's all. This time I had the sense: "Now I've got you! Now I've broken through. You're mine!" It felt wonderful. This was a gift.

I guess I needed these angels to visit me in a way that I would actually remember. I can only say that they were loving—loving in a sense that they knew me absolutely, totally—and I have felt just that much less alone and more complete ever since. Just their presence meant so much to me. They cared enough to appear, just to let me know they were here for me…that I'm not alone. Everything's been easier since then. Now I know I have angels.

—BILL SCHUMANN, SANTA BARBARA, CALIFORNIA,
ARCHITECT, WILDERNESS GUIDE

When you encounter an angel, you don't find another world different from your own, but a more real and true one within you.

As we free ourselves from our human ego, we discover our own essense as great spiritual beings, beautiful, angelic spirits with no purpose but to love. Our egos have their own agendas—to control, to seek power, love, and survival. But without ego in charge, we already have those things easily, naturally. We fly—we float in life. We feel we have it all. And we live angelic lives. It is the ego that trips us up, convinces us to desperately fight for what's already ours.

Angels don't need to take up arms, beg, or posture. They have wings to sail over and through difficulties. The only real escape from our own troubles is into the Infinitude of our real angelic soul nature.

It is our privilege to seek the thread of light that unites and protects and cares for us despite death, despite suffering and the seeming horrors that exist.

When you've tried everything else, and seen life fail your biggest tests, finally by default you turn in the one direction you would never have thought to look: inside. Not into the pain—that's only another exploration into the world of the mind and emotions, another search that must ultimately fail—but deeper.

THE MOST BEAUTIFUL SOUND

Many years ago I attempted suicide. At the time my life seemed hoplessly empty. Fortunately, I was brought to a nearby hospital just in time and received medical attention. However, my will to live was gone, and the staff could not do much for that. Lying alone in bed that night all I could do was repeat to myself, "I don't want to live, I don't want to live," when suddenly an unfamiliar voice called out to me. "Annette," he said, "I love you."

It was the most beautiful sound I had ever heard. Simple words, yet spoken so strong and true. At that moment I knew my life had purpose, I knew I was being loved and cared for by my angel.

—ANNETTE (*LAST NAME WITHHELD*)

Angel encounters prove to us that no matter what has happened to us or what we've done in the past, at any time, we can accept the personal, unconditional support of our angels and achieve great things.

To grow closer to your angels, inch closer to your "angelself." Move ever closer to God. Put your arm through His. Put your face in His hands. Sit in His lap and relax to your heart's content.

Angels speak to our souls in visions of light, in the painless resurrection of true happiness, in the simplicity of silence.

When we are willing to live as adults in childlike spiritual surrender, we are nurtured and cared for so sweetly.

THE BAR OF LIGHT

My wife and I had just separated, and I went home for Christmas to visit my mother in North Carolina. I went to my father's grave to pray. While I was praying, all of a sudden there was a bar of light that came straight down through my body from above. There was a bright light above me. I felt it pick me up onto my tiptoes, and it also sucked in my waist and threw out my chest. It was as if someone stuck a shiny metal bar straight from the top of my head down through my body, and then heat radiated out from that. The feeling of this bar of light was the most wonderful, warm feeling like nothing that you can get from a heating pad. It was from inside. It was wonderful. It was really wonderful.

I knew this was a spiritual experience, so I started praising God. And then I thought, "Geez, maybe He wants to say something, so I'd better shut up." So I shut up and quietly started listening, and I heard just one word but I heard it very clearly. It said, "Rest." And then in three or four seconds, the force, whatever it was, let me go, and I stood back down on my feet.

So I tried to feel the light again. I'd go back there every day because the experience was so great, but it didn't happen for

190

several days. Then one day it picked me up again—not as strong, but just the same. And it said just one word, "Go." It let me down, and I got terribly anxious to go back to California right away to try to reconcile with my wife.

I'd always prayed to have a personal experience with the Lord, that I would have a personal experience where I might see an angel. I didn't see a figure or anything like that. But I think it happened because I was praying there at my father's grave. It was very personal. I have been told many times that I have angels guarding me. I believe that now.

—CHARLEY NORTON, NORTH HOLLYWOOD, CALIFORNIA,
WRITER AND DIRECTOR

When we pick up the cosmic telephone and Someone says, "Hello," there is no longer any doubt in our minds of the reality of our Connection. When we pray and events change, when our point of view alters, when our intentions became transformed and our behavior is different, when the actions of others become more supportive or we have a private miracle, we can no longer deny that we have been answered. Then there is no force on earth that can create much doubt for us ever again.

Our assignment becomes: to open the connection, call more often, try to stay on the line a little longer the next time. We begin to think about what we want to ask for, how to be of greater use to the Divine, and how to ask for the job we really want. Because we know Someone is listening.

191

Although many people are wildly searching for something to believe in, the search has not ended when we discover angels. Angels are only the advertisement, not the goal.

❖ ❖ ❖

Angels offer hope. Not each of us will receive a physical healing, miracle, or rescue when we want it, but a spiritual one.

Intention and sincerity are everything to God—that means telling our real feelings. If we are covering up our negativity with positivity, the negatives can still win. Real spirituality includes the totality of who we are—not just the surface part that shows up in church or temple, or in dutifully caring for loved ones, sending money, calling once a week, giving gifts on holidays, keeping the kids in school or diapers.

God and the angels care about what's "wrong," too. Heaven doesn't want us to be prisoners of "niceness," being depressed or getting cancer as a final means of escape. God can't work with what we're hiding. He can only work with us to the degree we're willing to reveal ourselves to Him.

Test your faith by being ruthlessly honest with yourself, first. Admit to God just what it is that hurts, what you want, what you need. And then let go. Allow yourself to be taken care of. Allow the healing to take place. Affirm that you can have what you need and that everything in His hands is perfect. Accept the miracle. Then watch it unfold.

The mind is not needed to unravel or figure out Truth. It only gets in the way. Let it become quiet, and comprehend reality with your soul. In your quest for the Divine, don't be concerned with having company, with opinions, with where you fit in. Never be afraid of being alone when it is for soul research.

When we travel in Divine harmony with our angels, we see ourselves, and others as well, without labels, without lurking motives, without fear. We soften, gently detaching ourselves from problems and hardened attitudes, yet feeling new life flowing and discovering new solutions—freer ways of being.

Like bells and trumpets, violins, cellos, flutes, and drums, the angels' voices resonate throughout our souls and play into our lives.

Our hearts cannot contain all our love, for we are human. Grace expands us to receive the greater realms of love. Only in the realm of spirit do our highest feelings live and breathe. We cannot hold the light with a mere human grip. The light holds us.

THE MUSICAL VISIT

On March 15, 1993, my daughter Brianna died ninety-seven minutes after her birth. She had been born thirteen weeks prematurely with severe complications. I believe that on July 15, the angels brought her back to comfort me.

Last Christmas, my mother bought my baby a duck wearing a Santa Claus hat and a green scarf, and if you squeeze his beak, he plays "Jingle Bells." She gave it to me when I was four months pregnant as a gift for my unborn child.

The four-month anniversary of Brianna's death hit me the hardest. I was feeling so despondent and so sorry for myself. I never felt this way before or since. I was at home by myself, sitting on my bed, holding her picture and just crying, when all of a sudden the duck started to play "Jingle Bells." The duck is on a shelf on the other side of my room, no one was in there with me, and like I said, you must squeeze his beak for him to play.

Later that day, as I drove through the gates of the cemetery where she is buried, my digital car stereo jumped stations to the middle of a song that goes, "I'll be there," and I was struck by the part where it goes, "I'm on your side and I still care. I may have died but I've gone nowhere. Just think of me, and I'll be there." Then the radio went back to the original station it had been on.

That night, my mother and I were walking up the hall, and as we got to my bedroom door, we could hear "Jingle Bells" playing again. It has never happened again.

So, yes, I believe with all my heart that Brianna's angels brought her back to comfort me at a time when I desperately needed comfort the most. It has never happened again, but I have never been like I was that day.

I hope that my story will offer comfort to others who are faced with the death of a loved one. Maybe they, too, will realize, as I now do, that as long as they are remembered and kept alive in our hearts, they will always be with us.

—KIMBERLY DELUCA, TOMS RIVER, NEW JERSEY, CASHIER AT RESORTS CASINO IN ATLANTIC CITY

Unfortunately, it's no secret why many "bad" things happen. But for the mysterious traumas we experience, we must seek more mysterious answers. It is our privilege to explore the realms of cause and effect, the deeper laws that affect us, just as surely as the obvious ones. We can make use of the power of Heaven through our prayers and well-directed efforts.

When tragedy strikes, it is our job to be receptive to the healing of our wounds, to open our minds and our hearts to the love pouring down to us from the heavens. This love is capable of cleansing us of poisoned thoughts, infected feelings, and even impurities in our bodies.

Angels speak to us, like Mother Nature herself, who stares at us daily, wide-eyed like a mother lost in the love of her child, through every flower and tree, cloud and bird...always praying, "Be loving, be kind to your brothers; do not forget the essence of Heaven within me, for I am yours."

In cities, on the seas, in the forests, and in quiet places of the heart, seen, it is thought, only by small creatures, our memories, and the gentle sun's rays, the angels attend our cherished and private moments as well.

The angels capture us in weavings of love, giving light and warmth to our hardened feelings. In bitterest rage, in deepest grief, or loftiest grace we are all innocent children before their loving eyes.

Angel encounters reveal the precious moments when our limited beliefs about life are shattered by a greater awareness of unconditional love and kindness that surrounds us. In that instant our hopes are answered, our dreams are verified, our wishes for security and safety beyond our wildest dreams are fulfilled. We are spoken to in such a way that we finally relax into who we are. We receive a remedy to sorrow that could last throughout our lives. When we pray, now it is with certainty that we are being heard; when we speak, it is with a new clarity.

However briefly, we have witnessed the mechanics of destiny and the power of love. We have been given a new searchlight with which to see in darker passages of ourselves and a new license to hunt goodness, to scout for miracles, and to love the Giver forever.

Angels are gentle, subtle forces that allow us the total freedom we are used to having in everything else. The gifts we receive from them are the ones we earn by our receptivity.

BROKEN BONES

I first came in contact with angels after I suffered a very severe accident in Mexico. I had gone down to Puerto Vallerta on a holiday weekend with a girlfriend. We were in a taxi that crashed, and I suffered multiple fractures. The bones in my face were broken, my neck was broken, and I had a fractured left elbow. I lost a great deal of tissue at the elbow area, so I had to have skin grafted. And there were numerous fractures in my right arm. I had thirty-seven bones broken altogether. I was fractured like a potato chip.

The car had rolled over me, so I had gone out the window. I had a maxillary "T" fracture of the jaw, which is from one side to the other side and across the roof of my mouth. I was knocked unconscious, and they took me to this little house that was in the countryside. It was a place where they brought women to have their babies and then they went home, kind of an emergency stopping place before going to a hospital. I was there for several days, but they never took me to a hospital. I don't think they thought I was going to live. I was pretty scary-looking.

Still, I didn't have any fear. There was no fear about dying. I was totally conscious from the time I awoke from the accident and I had a lot of patience. I was very alert, and I felt very peaceful the whole time.

I couldn't call anybody; I couldn't move. The American consulate was closed. The lady I was traveling with was unable to locate anybody to help us right away. She had difficulty reaching anybody in the States. But a week later, we did get a born-again Christian man who was in charge of Western Airlines to agree to fly me back if I could walk on board, which is what I did. I didn't have any broken bones in my legs or hips, so I was able to do that, but, believe me, it was a very queasy kind of feeling.

When I got back to the States, they brought me to a hospital in California. I had about a hundred X rays, and they kept finding more fractures. I didn't have any feeling in my hand. I learned that if my hand hadn't been packed with mud

during the course of the accident, I would have bled to death.

I was in the hospital for about two months. It was very hard for me. I could not ask anybody for help. I was new to California, with a brand-new job. I didn't know many people. I didn't want to bother my family out of state. I did not have a support system. I did not know how to reach out. I don't know why, but that was part of my personality. I'd always think to myself, "I can do this by myself. I don't need help." I thought my determination was part of what was going to help me heal, but when it became very painful emotionally and physically, at a certain point I gave up. I totally gave up.

I actually made the decision: "I'm not going to do this any longer. It is too much for me. I am done." And one day I fell in a heap on the floor. I simply sat there, without moving, for days. Then I had a very, very strange experience….I was sitting on the floor, leaning back against my overstuffed chair, surrendered and thoughtless. I just had given up. I hadn't eaten anything in two days.

I heard this clear, authoritative voice that told me that all my pain was being removed, emotionally and physically, and that I would have twelve angels to help me. And for some reason, all I thought to ask was "What about this scar on my arm?" I was communicating with this voice, and I thought, "Oh, now I'm losing my mind." But this voice said, "You will always have a scar to remind you of this experience. The rest of the pain will be gone." It said, again, that I would have twelve angels to use for the rest of my life, at any time that I wanted.

I really felt I might be hallucinating. But all the pain in my body was gone. It was absolutely amazing to me that there was

suddenly no more physical or emotional suffering whatsoever. I felt as light as a feather. I didn't feel elated or anything like that. I felt peaceful. It was just…instant. I felt like there was somebody there with me.

Good things started happening for me at that point. I healed in a hurry. And all my needs began to be met in effortless ways. Physically, today, I'm great. My grip is 100 percent. In both arms. In fact, they told me I would never have full use of either one of my arms, but I do. The whole thing was a spiritual experience. I couldn't call it anything else. It was a turning point for me in all aspects of my life. I was no longer under any emotional stress or pressure of any kind, and the physical pain was completely gone. I felt powerful.

The experience was so profound that when I recovered, I quit my job and started my own business, a mobile notary public service. I didn't want to work for anyone anymore. I'm my own boss. And I'm never without a customer. I don't use my angels very often unless I really need them. I don't abuse them, you might say. When I wanted more freedom, I said, "I need a new job, and if I really, really do have angels, I don't have to go look for one. One will come to me." And it did.

My magical days are every day. If I have an extra expense during the month, maybe like automobile insurance, I end up having extra work that month. It just happens; I don't go after it. It just comes to me. I don't live my life with as much control. I live it with a lot more confidence and not as much manipulation on my part about what to do and how I'm doing. I don't worry as much.

I had always tried to do everything on my own and I finally

gave that up. This change is something that just happened. It was a catharsis. It was an intelligence that spoke to me. I believe there is an intelligence guiding me, and I choose to call these guiding things angels.

And each time if I talk about angels to somebody, it is almost as if I am smiled upon, because something nice happens for me.

I think it was almost a whole year before I told anybody this story because I didn't want to be doubted. I don't have any curiosity about who they are or what the voice is. I just accept that it's there. I don't exaggerate anything because I don't need to add any glamour to this experience.

I radiate an energy now that people like to be around. I am able to close my eyes and generate the feeling of total peace anywhere and anytime.

There is a natural peacefulness that comes with an association with angels. That's one of the angels' little bonuses.

I've even been able to help other people learn how to do it. The planet really needs to have some angelic serendipity, and we definitely need more peace.

—MARY MADDOX, SANTA MONICA, CALIFORNIA, MOBILE NOTARY PUBLIC

The energy of healing comes from a source outside the speculative images and hard concepts we are accustomed to. The inner music we hear comes from beyond the literal. The joy we feel blooming in our solitude is the response of a Supreme generosity, a singular compassion, an epiphany of kindness, inviolable, nameless, uncompromised.

The modesty and the exuberance of the Divine are like silent lightning streaking through our dark thoughts, like a white-hot sun spinning through us, cleansing all iniquities, a fire of infinite speed and cunning burning up our madness, yet painless and gratifying, gentle and all-loving.

Eminently awakening, unavoidably challenging and revealing, our new life with the angels is the thrilling predecessor to absolute peace.

It's quite right to get down on your knees and say, "God, angels, saints, I'm yours, guide me. I love you with all my heart. Heal me." And then to get up, healed.

Their compassion, like their joy, is the oceanic kind, with all the creatures of the deep within it. They challenge us to flight…like birds.…"Come with me!"

To be with the angels, give yourself much credit for all your courage to look where most people don't …into the the heart of things.

THE ROSE

My mother passed away in April 1994. We were very close.

She had been ailing with numerous health problems and had to go on dialysis in March. Mother was in the hospital for a month when we had to place her in a nursing home. We thought she was doing pretty well. She was in the nursing home three days when I walked into her room that last Sunday to find her taking her last breath.

I was in shock. I laid my head on her forehead crying, "Mom, when you get where you're going, please send me a rose."

My dear friend Eileen came by that evening. We sat down for some tea. I noticed she had a large shopping bag. A minute later, she reached in and pulled out a beautiful pink rose. I couldn't speak for a moment. When I told Eileen what I had said to my mother, she cried.

I feel my mother sent that rose...and she chose Eileen to give it to me. I had a lovely, warm feeling, and for the first time since the moment she died, I felt at peace.

Since then, I have been writing poetry, which I never did before in my entire life. Many people say my mother is helping me. I have always believed in angels. But now, it's nice to know that my mother is with them.

—MARILYN LOUISE RUSSO, PEN ARGYL, PENNSYLVANIA

Why don't angels rescue all the time? It is not their job. Angels take direction from a greater plan; they are part of the divine order that includes death and our free will.

To the angels, death is only another experience like so many others they have shared with you already.

❖ ❖ ❖

There is no shortage of angels for the person intimately open to the Divine, no loneliness, no fear of failure, no judgment or rejection. There is peace and a limitless feeling of freedom. You know you can fly if you want to. You know everyone can.

An angel encounter is a purposeful experience of loving and being loved. The sky can tell you about it. And the earth. So can water. And even fire loves to speak of it.

THE ANGEL ALTAR

I'm living in a little camper because of the earthquake. It's ironic. I have a two-story house, and I do hand-painted furniture. And everything in the house and also on the walls fell to the floor. The earthquake shook our house so badly that our front double doors, which were double-dead-bolt-locked, were forced off their jambs. Even the doors to the oven fell off and crashed to the floor. All the books, all the bookshelves, everything standing landed on the floor.

Except one little area halfway upstairs to where my office and bedrooms are, on the landing, that is my angel place. I have a hand-painted bench there, and I have a little cup and saucer, and I have my baker's rack with my little angel collection and my angel books. It is a place for me to sit and be with the angels. I have angel pictures on the wall. The area up there was the only spot in the whole house that still had pictures up. My husband had gotten me a beautiful angel snow globe for Christmas that plays music. It was on a glass shelf, which didn't break, either; nothing of my angel collection broke. Even though the quake was so strong that it knocked the wrought-iron railing off the wall—that was how forceful it was—don't you think it would have at least knocked my angel pictures off the wall?

When the city inspector came, he looked at the house and he said, "By all rights, you should have been killed in your bed. The chimney was loose, and a few seconds more you wouldn't have made it." As he walked up the stairs, he saw my angels sitting there. He stood there and—the hair on the back of his neck was standing on end…he said, "Everything is down in your house except for the angels. Did you put these back up?" And I said, "No, these remained standing." We both knew that everything on that one little landing in the stairwell between the first and second stories, realistically, should have fallen.

As a child, I was very demanding. And this is one of the things that I still do. I still say, "Prove it to me; send me a sign." I don't think God, the Higher Power, has the time to really send me signs. I think I can direct my requests to the angels, because that's what I think they're there for. I think God has more important things to deal with than to prove to Carol Donnelly

that something is going to happen or to send her a sign. I always direct my requests to the angels. I really do. I say, "This is my problem…I need some guidance and I really want you to send me a sign." And I get them all the time.

—Carol Donnelly, Simi Valley, California, entrepreneur, artist, songwriter, fashion designer, and actress

A dozen angels could wake up an atheist in the middle of the night and dance on his stomach and he'd explain the whole thing another way. We're subject to the experiences our conditioning prescribes, perceiving our lives according to our own definitions. Angels are respectful of our self-imposed limitations. Therefore we will never find a reality beyond our own, a more supreme one, unless we ask, unless we release our own limited concepts and attitudes. Then we are ready to receive it.

When we start to understand what angels are, we start to notice the results of angelic presences everywhere.

Imagine yourself to be serving the holiest of beings when you serve your fellows. Keep nothing back when you feel enlightened by love for a passing friend or moved to lend a hand. Take all the joy you can from your experiences with others. Let love come straight from your heart.

As aspiring angels ourselves, we feel love for our fellow beings, for creatures and children, for the wonders of nature, for teachers, students, and friends.

None of us have to be so special to help the angels or be helped by them. We just need a little bit of faith.

HOSPITAL PRAYER

One month before Woodstock, I was on the corner of Fourteenth Street and Eighth Avenue in New York City at twelve noon, waiting for the light to change. And a great big guy comes up to me and sticks an eighteen-inch knife in my chest. I fell back onto the ground. I thought he punched me. So I went to punch him, and all of a sudden, I see blood gushing. I didn't know he put a knife in me. Then I went into shock.

Before I knew it I was in the hospital and my lungs were filling up with blood. They had to operate. Afterward, I was lying in bed; I was in a ward with six people whom they just scraped off the ground. And I was lying there with my eyes closed and I heard a priest—I was in St. Vincent's Hospital in New York in the Village—I hear a priest giving someone the last rites, and I thought it was me. I'm thinking while I'm asleep, I'm thinking, "Here I am, a Jewish kid, you know, and I'm dead, and I got a priest giving me the last rites." At least I knew my mind was working. But I finally get my eyes open, and it's the guy next to me who died. I was very happy it wasn't me. But, you know, I

had tubes coming out of me, with pumps and stuff.

So about two days later there was a kid in the next ward who had gone through a plate-glass window. There was a 99-percent chance that they were going to have to amputate his leg because gangrene was setting in. They just didn't think they could save it. But five days later, when I could move around a little bit, the kid asked if I'd go to church with him and pray for him.

I really liked this kid; there was something about him. So I said, "Sure." So I went down to the chapel, and I sat through the whole service. But the kid couldn't stop asking me to please pray for him. He said, "I know you can save my leg." And I said, "Why?" He said, "I feel that's why I met you." So I went back into the chapel and sat for two hours, praying. I suppose it's sacrilegious, but I even took the little biscuit on my tongue. I mean, I really focused in on this kid. Never saw the kid again afterward, but they didn't have to operate on his leg. Next day they came and told me they thought there was a good chance they could save it. When I left the hospital, in another week, he was okay.

My getting stabbed was like, inconsequential. I really felt like I was in the hospital to help the kid save his life. I guess I was an angel. I was sent. I believed.

—STANLEY NEWTON, VENICE, CALIFORNIA,
PROFESSIONAL PHOTOGRAPHER

The "poor, handicapped, and needy" may be the very hiding places for the Divine Ones. They will awaken your sense of trust, self-worth, and well-being more than any kingly gift or

promise of fame. Don't be predjudiced for or against any "kind" of personality because that is the cheap view of life. To know that there are angels around you will make you richer and wiser than you could ever imagine—and more safe than you have ever felt before.

Sometimes, in spite of our own limited thinking, we surprise ourselves and leap into the cosmic river and catch a fish. We experience a miracle, or take part in one…one that we can savor until the day we die.

Angel appearances, like all true miracles, strengthen our faith and encourage us to remember that we are part of the eternal family and are therefore unconditionally loved.

THE KISS

I have had an angel encounter. I was going through the darkest time in my life. I had just graduated from high school and found out that I was pregnant. I decided to have an abortion. The night before was very difficult for me, and I was scared. I couldn't sleep, but then I felt a soft kiss on my cheek. Not many people believe me, but I know it was an angel. Afterward, I was able to sleep that night. What I did was the right thing for me, but I was glad to know that an angel was there with me. I hope that I can become an angel to others because there are so many angels in my life.

—NAME WITHHELD

Angels are universal in their healing. They have no need to divide and conquer. They shower us all, equally, with love.

Angels can be appreciated once in a lifetime or as a daily experience. Our holy mentors can be all but forgotten or constantly remembered. That is up to us.

ANGEL TOUCH

I sometimes feel angels brush my hair. It feels like a light touch on the side of my face, sometimes on the back of my hair, on my head, sometimes at the front of it. Sometimes there's a message, but often it's just letting me know that they are there. Other times I get messages without this happening at all.

I think of them as either angels or guides. I generally find them in two situations: If I'm going through a difficult period, something heavy, the angels come in and tell me I'm not alone. Second, they sometimes want me to notice a particular coincidence. I may be looking at a billboard or hearing a song on the radio that applies to me, or looking at a certain person with whom I need to resolve feelings, or when somebody is saying something to me that could help me grow, and they want me to pay attention to that particular thing.

—*NEIL (JONAH) ANDERSON, ASHLAND, OREGON*

These wise beauties relish and caress us with more grace than we ever dream.

Sometimes we feel embarrassed by our needs. We think that society will disapprove if we admit our weaknesses or our anger. We try to please the world, but we deny ourselves when we deny

our spiritual emptiness or suppress our grief and anger over the lack of meaning in our lives, our feelings of separateness from others. Being carried along by habit, social rules, and family duty can make us spiritual cripples, psychological glass houses awaiting the inevitable stone.

We have to trust the inevitable laws of Heaven more than our own methods of keeping out of trouble. It's just like sailing in a boat being tossed on a rough sea. When you point your sail into the wind, all becomes calm. When you tell the truth—whatever it may be—you move to the calm eye of the hurricane, you find the diamond inside the piece of coal, the full moon waiting for you behind the cloud.

Telling the truth requires faith that what you really want can become a reality for you. The truth is a miraculous place where all things are possible. Faith is the stuff that will ultimately set us totally free, where all that is good and right is constantly fulfilled, because there is no lack within.

Without an inner commitment to the holy force within that seeks to assist and love us, we slip back into the materialistic mentality that gives us nothing but disappointment, ultimately.

When we want to be with angels, we can move out of our heads and into our hearts, drop the charade of "knowing it all," seek higher guidance than the limited instructions of our youth or our overburdened intellects. We can distinguish between magicians, devils, ghosts, charlatans, and angels. We become smart and

single-mindedly devoted to the truth, whatever that may be.

Angels don't challenge or confront us. No one waves a finger in our face and scolds us. No one yells in our ears. Angels aren't like that.

When we find our own incentive to discover the Holy Presence, our insatiable urge for happiness is what carries us....

As human beings we can emulate angels or devils; we can be anything we want to be.

Include them in your circle of friends. Address angels daily and let them address you. Teach your children about them. Share your angel stories with other people.

BLACKOUTS TO LIGHT

I used to be a major alcoholic. My guardian angel's a female. Her name is Elizabeth Marie Katlyn. Well, that's the name that came to me, that's all. I talk to her every morning. Before I met her, I was praying and telling God, "You know, I never had an angel experience or a miracle to prove Your presence or anything." And all of a sudden, a voice came out of my head, and it said, "Yeah, who do you think led you out of all of those blackouts you had?" And I started crying. I just started crying. I had never even thought of it. The hundreds of blackouts I had.

Who protected me? That's all the voice said.

I mean I'd be driving heavy drunk so many times and I'd end up at home somehow, or I'd wake up in the car somewhere, safe. In one three-month blackout I had, I'd wake up every morning somewhere else. I never knew where I was. Yeah, it's amazing how divinely protected and guided I was. It's amazing! Yep. Now, I believe. I'm thinking that the universe is really user-friendly.

I tattooed a big beautiful angel on my forearm because when people ask me about it, I remember that they're an angel. And when I drive, I'm always looking at it. She's always there, my inner…I mean, this is my inner angel of light.

I did a guardian angel meditation with the women inmates in a prison near here. There wasn't a dry eye in the group. I mean, they just opened up. They said what their angels said to them, and what they told them to do. One woman couldn't even talk she was just so choked up. Well, most of the guys have tattoos and they were looking at my angel, and they said, "Oh, that's one of them paste-on things." And I said, "No, it's not." There's thirteen different colors in it. So I tell 'em, "Well, that's what we are, we're all angels of light!"

Just changing their thinking is what I'm trying to do. That's what it takes; it's just only a thought, and a thought can be changed.

—JERRY DOYLE, GREENBACKVILLE, VIRGINIA,
DRUG AND ALCOHOL COUNSELOR

When we know angels, we finally face which part of us it is that lives and which that dies, which love to cling to and which

215

to let go, what noble desires underlie our great desires and which foolish yearnings. We know with certainty what great Being it is which guides us, or ego, sadly, wastes us.

Decide to be your own angel. Pledge to yourself that you will hold the Divine hand within you and that you will never let it go.

Never let what is good be crushed by doubt or self-punishment. Never accept evil thoughts like failure and inner insincerity. This is you cutting your ties with your angels. Self-hate and self-condemnation are very difficult to get through because they are so opaque. It is a hiding place, a negative retreat in the dark, where angels are not allowed.

Decide to walk through all the dark forests of confusion and doubt on your way into the light with the secure footing of one who walks with angels. Be a simple soul full of grace. Stand tall and radiantly among your peers. Teach children and elderly alike about the treasures of love and of angels.

If angels truly walked the earth, human beings would know them only by their deeds. For the angels' presence is just like ours when we are at our very best. Angels walk among us, never calling attention to themselves, reflecting that which is Divine in each of us, like courage, selflessness, love.

They appeal to our higher senses through gestures of comfort

216

and encouragement, through feelings of peacefulness and of play.
They teach us by example, calling on us through humor and
demonstrations of extraordinary will, through an unflinching
and divinely impassioned commitment to love. They call to our
greater intelligence, our vastest inspiration, our compassion, and
our simple faith.

Angels rejoice in our generosity and frolic in our positivity.

❖   ❖   ❖

Angels evoke spiritual memories of indescribable tenderness
and well-being.

If Heaven has a face, it shines in saintly splendor, beaming
love, ruling oceans, turning us toward Heaven with a wink.

THE BEST FRIEND

I have always felt very spiritual, yet it wasn't until four years ago
that I really realized the amazing power of angels. I was only
fifteen years old, and I lost one of my best friends, Brady, in a car
accident. Being so young this event seemed incomprehensible. I
felt lost, not knowing how I was ever going to be able to finally
let go and say good-bye.

A few nights after her death, I was lying in bed, trying to
comprehend the loss I felt. Brady then appeared to me, her body

illuminated with light and love. It was almost like a dream, although I know that I was not dreaming. I was crying to her, asking her why she had to leave. She told me that she was all right and that this was where she was supposed to be now. We embraced, and as I opened my eyes I could still feel the presence of her arms around me. For a long time, I did not know how to comprehend this experience. All I knew was that I had never felt so at peace and so delighted with God as I did at that moment. It wasn't until six months later that I was once again visited by Brady.

It was the night before her sixteenth birthday, when I was once again sitting in my room, thinking about her. We had had our last birthday party together, and I felt sadness knowing that we would not be able to share another birthday party together ever again. Then I heard a soothing voice say to me, "You did not lose a friend but, instead, gained an angel." That sentence seemed so appropriate and made so much sense to me that ever since then I have collected angels. I truly believe that Brady is now one of my guardian angels.

Brady has touched me through many other experiences and probably more than I realize, but most recently I felt compelled to visit Brady's grave. I meditated for a short time, asking her to guide me and show me what it was that I have to do this summer. That afternoon I began drawing angels. I have now drawn more than fifty angels. It feels good, and it makes me think of Brady and all my other angels I hope to meet one day. This is another place that Brady has led me.

So here I am. I feel once again led by angels to write you this letter, which I normally would never do.

—NAME WITHHELD

Friendship is merely an affirmation of the loving being we really are. Through love we experience our infinitude. Through love we extend into everything, and everything extends through love into us.

This world was not meant for us to hold on to. It isn't a punishment or a flaw in the construction of the world, but a gift. Because we are freer than that. Where we hang our hat for the moment is not the ultimate. The ultimate has no limits at all. And when you get there, you throw away all your hats, all your costumes, all your faces. You just come as you are.

In truth we are all much closer than we have formerly imagined. Our hearts are a part of one another not only here but on the other side as well. We are blessed by the many friends we all have—forever.

We can never be abandoned. We can never be alone or left out. None of us can. The angels provide the proof. We can seek and find the thread that unites and protects us all despite the seeming horrors that exist. Despite the fact of death.

Our relationship with angels is not determined by proximity or history, memories or actions. We don't know them because of blood, common interests, or any physical thing.

Awareness of angels brings its own rewards. The longer we

wait to unburden ourselves of our own negativity, the longer we suffer with our own insecurity and the symptoms of it. The sooner we surrender to the Divine, the sooner we heal.

HEART AWAKENINGS

I do heart-awakening sessions. I have developed a way of working with the angelic realm to assist people. I allow the angels to take control of my hands; they are always invited into the session. The person is put on the table and is just surrounded by them. It's like a wall of light that surrounds the table.

I think the first time I saw an angel was about a year ago. There was a figure in my bedroom doorway. It was about six feet tall and had this absolutely brilliant white face. It was just incredible. It was a form of white light and energy.

When I do a session, angels come into the room. We can feel the energy of them. All of a sudden, everybody's all hooked into the Holy Spirit. Then I'm on autopilot as far as what I do. It just happens automatically. Different angels come in and work through my hands. I let go and my hands will do all these weird things. I allow angels to come into my aura. That's a very exhilarating feeling. And at times I can see them.

Sometimes I'll request a specific angel, like Archangel Michael or Archangel Uriel or Archangel Rafael and sometimes, also, Jesus. There are other angels who show up, too, various specialists in different things. I speak to them. They will tell me different things I need to do, like if I need to put my

hands on a person at a different place, where I need to do it and for approximately how long.

The other day a woman felt an angel's hand on her stomach. She thought it was my hand, but my hands weren't even on her. She said, "That wasn't your hand on my stomach? I looked up and your hands weren't on me. But a hand was there."

You have to surrender yourself, to just flow. Sometimes, in the sessions, I've been told to do something ridiculous. One time, an elderly lady came who had a frozen shoulder from falling down some concrete stairs. Her shoulder couldn't be moved for over a year. First I did some work on her shoulder with my hands. And then I was told to put my hands on her head. I said, "This is ridiculous! I am not doing this. This is utterly ridiculous and it's not going to help her shoulder!" And I was told, "You will be pleased with the results." So, finally, I knew it was all done and had her move her shoulder. Sure enough, her arm went straight up. She broke down and cried. Her entire problem had vanished.

I believe that in the angelic realm, there is no limitation. There is all love.

—CHUCK ALTEN, SCOTTSDALE, ARIZONA, MECHANICAL ENGINEER WHO
DESIGNS JET ENGINES AND PART-TIME HEALER

It is our right to learn about love, angels, death, Heaven, God. And no matter what anyone says to us, from what pulpit or platform, it is ultimately our own job to open the door to the heavenly realms ourselves, and to walk through that door under

our own steam, on our own terms. Only when we do that will we really know that we have been surrounded by angels all along and just how free and yet how entirely protected we really are.

Knowing our angels, we become more at home in the realm where there is no fear...Heaven.

It isn't necessary to try to hear things you don't hear or see things you don't see, but to encounter more angels, try to open your intuition to the greater harmony of life. Get to know the angelic parts of yourself.

❖　❖　❖

The love we cherish never ends. Certainly not with death. To know, as the angels do, the limitlessness of love, we must rise to the occasion, expand beyond our fears and out of our own limited ways of thinking in order to own it.

THE PEOPLE IN THE LIGHT

A six-year-old boy was playing in his driveway when the garage door fell on his head. He was rushed to the hospital, near death. When he came to, his parents sat him down to explain to him what had really happened. The kid said, "I already know."

And the parents asked, "How do you know?"

"The people told me," he answered.

"What people?" his parents asked.

"The people in the light," the boy said.

"What people?"

"The people who told me to stay, because I wanted to go. And they kept saying, 'Stay, stay, no, you need to stay.' And I kept saying, 'No, I want to go!'"

But he eventually decided to listen to the people, and he stayed and got better. Today, he is a perfectly healthy and happy child.

—AS TOLD BY A FRIEND OF THE BOY'S MOTHER

Where we put our attention is what we will attract. The more angel thoughts we put into children's heads, the more angels they will attract.

Angels are a part of our past, our present, a part of all circumstances, even a part of our future. When we look ahead, it is right to believe we will have angels then, too.

When, like children, we don't depend on our social conditioning, people's opinions, and other intellectual structures for our identity, there's so much more room for angels to penetrate our reality, to come into our souls and spread their wings.

THE MAN WHO GAVE OUT HUGS

Walt was leaving his office in downtown Santa Cruz with a lot of things on his mind. He was thinking about his Down syndrome child and the fact that he was having a lot of stress at work. On his way home, late in the day, he walked to the corner feeling very anxious and worried about all kinds of things. He was standing on the street corner waiting for the light to change when a man approached him. He appeared to be a street person. He was not especially dirty, just a bit bedraggled. The man walked up to him, looked him in the eye, and said, "You look like you need a hug." Walt was astonished. No words could have been more true at that moment. He couldn't even speak. Nothing like this had never happened to him, particularly when he needed it so badly.

There they were on the street corner, and this strange man gave him a hug. Walt said this hug was divine. It was not just a hug, it was an amazingly nurturing, helpful hug. He thought to himself, "This guy must be an angel. Where did he come from? You don't just have somebody come up and say, 'You need a hug?' The man's eyes just twinkled. His energy was so clean and pure. Walt actually accepted this wonderful hug, which was a long, releasing kind of hug, not the short, masculine version of a hug, and even thanked the guy, who then walked off into the crowd of pedestrians and disappeared.

Walt proceeded on his walk, and within three or four blocks he was absolutely floating. His energy had shifted, and he felt completely transformed by this angelic man. But as he continued on his way his worries returned. He had to go to the grocery store, he had to do this and that, and the huge pile of office work that had to get done later that night loomed in front of him. Besides all this, he also had to see the kids and have dinner and so on.…

Four blocks farther, standing at another traffic light, he was caught up in worries all over again when, out of the blue, the same man returned. He walked right up to Walt again, faced him, looked him in the eyes once more, and gently said, "You look like you need another hug." And he gave him another hug. Then he just disappeared. This time the message stuck. Walt was like "twinkletoes" the whole way home.

The angelic stranger reminded him once and for all that he was not alone. The universe was willing to give him a hug when he most needed it. This man occasionally appeared at other times, too. Always when Walt needed a lift. Walt considered the man an angel, and after getting past the man's unusual appearance the very first time, he always accepted the divine gesture of love he offered as a gift from above.

To this day, he has never forgotten the man who gave out hugs.

—WALT ALLEN, SANTA CRUZ, CALIFORNIA, LAND-USE PLANNER

Angels don't want credit. They are not attention seekers or media hounds. They are not seeking fame or publicity or recognition. They do not even seek love, because love is what they are.

The angels play the kind of music that no one else can hear, except for those in love.

This is what angels are for. To show us the glory that peeks at us through those very cracks in our understanding, where the light simply wants to shine on us…where God wants to gently speak to us, where Heaven simply wants to encompass us, to give us a tender hug and send us on our way.

❖ ❖ ❖

AMBER

I am an ordinary person who has had the most extraordinary experience. I have turned to God, I was a nonbeliever before. I used to laugh at people when they talked about religion. I used to mock them and make them stop talking about it in my house because I thought it was nonsense. I was a real gum-chewing, nail-filing girl who only wanted to shop her whole life away. It's a weird thing at thirty-two to be completely turned around like this.

I used to think you're like a refrigerator, you break down and they bury you in the ground. But when I started seeing the things I saw, I was overwhelmed. I was so excited I couldn't sleep for many nights, thinking about it.

Two days before Christmas, my husband, from whom I was separated, and I still weren't together. I was in the woods on a hill;

there is this big pointy rock that's kind of angular and it blocks the wind. I was in a quiet mood, just appreciating how beautiful it was. I grew up here. I've been here my whole life. I was sitting and thinking, and that is when I saw it. At first, when I saw her I didn't even know what I was seeing. It was a formless shape, a bright light....Then I saw the most beautiful thing I ever saw in my life.

The white was so white and her wings looked like the stomach on a duck—fine and soft and white. It was the most incredible thing I ever saw! It's not like you could have reached out and touched her. It was like a vision with your eyes open. Like she was somewhere else, but I saw her.

Then, several days later, I saw my grandfather. I remember I lay back on the bed as I was taking off my boots, and the figure was so vivid. I saw lots of people in my family I had never met. They had died before I was born. I was so shocked I told my father about it, and he confirmed everything. It just blew our minds. I started to realize for the first time in my life that there really is another place that people don't know about, and I was all full of inspiration! How could I go back to how I used to be? It's really amazing. My eyes are wide open. It's unbelievable!

And there's more than that. When I was around twenty, I had my first operation. I always had a problem with cysts. My recent one was really bad. This summer I had this really big thing. It just sat in there. The doctor drained many, many ounces of fluid. But it always came back. But the thing disappeared! It happened right when all of this started, in August. It's gone! I'm in perfect health. I remember right before this happened I was in bed and I was praying. I was trying everything. But the cyst kept coming back with my cycles. Since I saw

the angel, it's completely gone. No more pain! God healed me. It's an amazing thing.

My friends always said to me, "You have to believe in God," and I would tell them, "I can't." That's what I'd say to them.…*He* must have known I really needed to believe because that is when I saw the angel.

One day, I had to go to the emergency room for something, and while I was there, I took a walk and everybody I saw was suffering—I could feel it. I could feel what everyone was feeling, and I loved them. I was not a coldhearted person before, but I didn't really care, I was so shallow. And now I can *feel* people. My heart is…huge! I always want to do something to help people. I'm just bent on helping people.

I was given so many gifts. I'll never be the same selfish girl I used to be. I saw a beautiful angel. I was given visions of people that I never had a chance to meet! I was physically and spiritually healed. My husband and I are back together, and he is even starting to open up a little, like other members of my family. Not everybody. My mother believes everything is genetics. She's a bodybuilder and she thinks everything can be scientifically explained. She doesn't believe in miracles or anything like that. And neither does my grandmother. I see miracles happening around me all the time, though.…I mean everything is fine now. It's amazing. I can't say I've ever been this happy before.

—AMBER ALLEN, NEW JERSEY MOTHER

If you want drama, do something dramatically positive, radi-

cally pleasing, or remarkably wise. Attempt to do something movingly kind or shockingly beautiful. Forgive someone, forgive God, forgive the world, forgive yourself.

Shake off selfishness. Let go of anger. Pop the bubble of pride. Accept comfort if you're grieving. If you fear, accept safety. When you have a need, let go of the idea that there is an obstacle. Throw your request onto God's desk and accept that your order is already filled. This is how to work with the angels to help yourself grow.

Do an act of Divine intervention for someone. Give something to someone for no reason. Mentally accept one new person completely, every day.

Decide that you yourself will be the first angel always, to guard and guide you, to love and cherish you, to urge you to greater freedom.... Then see what comes along, what great angels cross your path.

The angels respond to our gratitude, finding their way into our hearts and our lives, through love. Angels never miss an opportunity to be close to us. The more we thank Heaven, the more gifts Heaven will bestow.

Happiness is really only this: our consciousness of unlimited goodness. Whether we are happy for a brief moment or a lifetime or an eternity depends on how conscious of this goodness we are willing to be.

III

Eternal Advice

Our angel encounters tell us that everything is possible. Nothing is hidden when we are open and courageous. Reveal yourself and thereby reveal the holy ones who will carry you to your goals. Take courage in the little things that happen to urge you on and let you know that you are on the right track. These are your own angel messages. What you have faith in has faith in you. When you remember that Heaven is with you, you will soon know what angels are. Take joy in good fortune, take courage in friendship. Know that you will never be abandoned no matter how things look, and promise never to abandon others who look to you for love.

Keep your chin up and your inner angel alive by being kind and recognizing the kindness of others. Keep faith when others doubt. Stay true to your own sense of fair play. Hang on to the realization that you are perfect, not in an ordinary sense but a divine one.

The angels ask that you invest of your spirit toward others in your gestures of goodwill and kindness. Give lavishly—give all you have—go for broke. Let the best of you come forth to shower on the most "insignificant" person you may find in your travels. Remember, they may be an angel who has come to offer

you special moments if only by receiving your love and allowing you to feel your own worthiness.

Stand like a beacon of compassion to the worthy and the undeserving alike. Smile into the eyes of all people. See how the nature of your life will change—no boredom anymore, but constant inspiration to love. You will be rewarded as angel after angel offers their gifts at your feet and places the heart of Heaven in your already open hands.

Angels love to flock to the honest and receptive ones among us, those who acknowledge the greater Truth and in so doing make the world a more beautiful place...to everyone who seeks to fill a need rather than seeking fulfillment at the expense of others...those simple heroes who inadvertently command such respect we blush in our attempts to be casual toward them.

Never be ashamed of what is in your own heart. All of creation grows on love. Be light. Be shining in your soul. Gather all hearts into your own and be faithful to your truer self. Remember the light within everything, which is God. Accept the goodness of the light—that it surrounds you and shines inside you. Accept everything as a part of this light. See how silly your own evil thoughts about yourself and others are, how only you suffer. See heavenly light surrounding everything you can think of...all your "problems," all people, the whole universe. This is a great angel meditation of happiness and joy...a very healing one. Like angels, see the light shining every-where, all the time.

Contact angels in whatever ways you can. Form a new rela-tionship in the Now. Feel free to ask all your questions, unburden yourself of all your worries, receive answers to your

questions directly from the angels' unique position. Don't hold anything back. Your holy friends will receive you unconditionally, in your entirety, and they can handle anything. The advice you receive will be priceless; the relationship you discover with them, perfect.

Never be bashful. Make open gestures of your love and goodwill and admit your faults as well as your good intentions. Let them come into your process of growing.

Let the angels guide you home. Know you do have a wonderful family and the very best of friends, neighbors, role models, counselors, playmates, soul mates. You have angels. And from the moment that you wish it, the angels have you.

There is an "angel" born every minute. Let the next one be you.

As you move through your days, and you go about living in the presence of angels, if no one sees or acknowledges your kindness, just say to yourself, "If I have pleased the angels today, that is enough."

When your mind tells you to do one thing but your heart tells you another, don't be blind to destructive forces, but listen to your heart. It knows best. Your mind seeks entertainment for itself. Your heart seeks the infinite treasures of love. Powerful people of the greatest intelligence may be running the earthly show, but one true heart will conquer even the greatest of minds.

Allow the angels to mold your heart. It is your job to lead your mind back again and again to the deeper chambers of your heart. Then, pay attention and do the will of your heart when it speaks to you. Like an angel, it will serve.

Celestial Prayer

My angels:

Help me to hear your heavenly instructions and wisdom....Come to me, on the clouds, in the sunlight, in the rivers, on the wind, in the forests, in the cities, in my home and in all homes, in all the streets, in all the fields, in all the towns, in the backyards and mountains of the world....Come to me in the skies in the night and in the morning, in the day and at the twilight hour; where human beings gather and where they do not; where nature takes its course and where people push and shove to find their way....Be always with me in every journey I embark on and in every friendship I invoke, in every course of study, every great dream and reality that I imagine....

Help me to hear the voice of the Divine, to know His will and kindness. Gather me up when I am lonely. Keep me humble as you reveal your humility in every flower, every passing rainbow, every centered song and angelic leap into love....

Heavenly Father, let us know, in our secret hearts, the rightness of all things. Give us the understanding heart that You have bestowed upon Your angels, that You invest in all newborn children and little creatures when they come into this world. Help us to find the purpose that will take us back to the days of trust and forgiveness when we had nothing on our minds but to enjoy the nearness of You and to relish the moments playfully given. Let us feel that happiness once again; unburden our hearts and minds in Your supreme grace.

My angels, I yearn to hold, caress, and love you—but an

angel is too free a thing for that. An angel is a shimmer, a spark, a puff, a ray. An angel can't be owned.

Is that you in my dreams?…The light that glows from behind the night images?…In the wind gliding over my arms, silky with your wings?…Is that you glistening in green leaves, in trees in the forest, in the grass and flowers? Are you bubbling in streams, in the rain splashing from the sky? Is that you I watch in the movement of the moon—slowly, catlike, and with perfect poise? Have I met you in my loves, in friends I greet each day? Have I known you all along?

I will wait for you, speak to you, think of you, and love you until I leave this earth and my soul can mingle with yours, a single breath of Spring, a like essence—singing and playing in the stars.

Ageless Encouragement

Whenever we unify ourselves inside with our angels, the love that exists within us reflects more and more in love all around us. We fear less. We think less. We know more. We become free. When we cry, we don't cry quite as despairingly, and when we laugh, it is with a more universal sense of joy. We see everything as less isolated and more unified.

The frightened stranger within each of us begins to realize there is nothing to fear, there is no reason to hide. It becomes more and more difficult to forget our Connections. And sweetest of all, we know there are wondrous beings of pure love, a galaxy

of angels who invisibly surround us, a comfort and blessing to all.

It is so urgent that we each know that we are not alone or forgotten, that our instincts have been right. Like when we were children and were ministered to by great presences who cared for us, clustered around us, who touched and lifted and held us, who played with us and kept us safe, applauded when we achieved a goal or merely revealed our innate sweetness, we are still similarly blessed. Even in adult life, we are surrounded by tremendously caring, profoundly powerful, highly enlightened beings.

As human beings, we need to know that when we're in trouble, thinking no one cares or sees, there are those who care very deeply. That when no one is cheering for us, though we achieve great things, there are splendid, magnificent beings

cheering and roaring their gladness for us.

They are laughing with us in the inner realms in our fun, at the fantastic miracle of living, winking their approval, patting our backs with an unseen hand, and kissing our little heads, thrilled right to the core with us at our bold daring to be happy, our courageous and energetic leaps into our freedom.

For the spiritually adventurous it is a delight to investigate angels. There is no distance or physical space to maneuver to find them. There are no difficult tasks to fulfill, no privileges to earn, no problems to overcome. Angels are right here, all the time, waiting for us to ask a real question, express a real need, so they can guide us to the answer in the unlimited realm of Perfection in which they live.

We naturally clean up our earthly act in many ways by surrendering to our angels as guides. Angels encourage us to live not only to get what we can before the ship sinks but to help repair the boat.

It is in times of doubt and darkness we need to know whose support we can count on—our own angels, living in a miraculous world of truth, beauty, and love surrounding us and inside us, invisibly....

Our relationship with angels will go on whether we are awake to their love or asleep, by our choice to know them or by default. With our permission or without, they will forever be our hidden friends or, if we so choose, our obvious companions. But by whatever mode they come, knowing about angels is highly liberating. They express the unlimited possibility of joy, continuous and never-ending.

There is nothing we cannot do; our greatest dreams can be

realized; our most beautiful goals can come true; our souls can express the Perfection whence they were born; our Source is our greatest friend and ally. We are never without love. We are always protected. We truly are free, right now.

Angels are an appealing appetizer to a delicious world of infinite happiness and cosmic thrill. Because the road that leads to angels leads beyond them, to the Eternal One, to perfect Peace and Freedom. With each step in this direction we gain better understanding of the ultimate Destination that is possible.

On earth, we learn to fly by curiosity, yearning to know what lies beyond our own definitions of things. When we have lost our own map to our destinies, we will do justice to our sense of freedom by recognizing the essential, magnificent Power that leads us.

Our desire for Heaven and Heaven's grace work together. Whenever we accept an inch in the heavenly realms, we are given a mile.

The beauty of the angels is great. We need nothing more. Even their music is secondary. We cannot hear it for the love.

Angels will always guide you to your real self—to the infinite beauty of your own heavenly soul—where there really isn't any pain or confusion, only infinite love and eternal joy. This is where the angels live. It isn't hurtful there. It's the only place of sanity there is. Imagine that. You go Home.

Angels prove that everything is possible. That miracles are possible. That life is a miracle. And that we are a miracle, too.

Everyone has an angel story.

If you have a miracle story of angels, healing, or faith you'd
like to share, I'd love to hear it. Please write to:

KAREN GOLDMAN

8721 SANTA MONICA BOULEVARD, #118

WEST HOLLYWOOD, CA 90069-4511